SHELL GUIDES

edited by JOHN BETJEMAN AND JOHN PIPER

CORNWALL
John Betjeman

DORSET
Michael Pitt-Rivers

HEREFORDSHIRE
David Verey

THE ISLE OF WIGHT
Pennethorne Hughes

LINCOLNSHIRE
Henry Thorold and Jack Yates

NORFOLK
Wilhelmine Harrod and C. L. S. Linnell

RUTLAND
W. G. Hoskins

SOUTH-WEST WALES
PEMBROKESHIRE AND CARMARTHENSHIRE
Vyvyan Rees

SUFFOLK
Norman Scarfe

WORCESTERSHIRE
James Lees-Milne

---

edited by JOHN PIPER

ESSEX
Norman Scarfe

NORTHUMBERLAND
Thomas Sharp

WILTSHIRE
J. H. Cheetham and John Piper

NORTHAMPTONSHIRE
Lady Juliet Smith

THE SHELL PILOT TO THE SOUTH COAST HARBOURS
K. Adlard Coles

NORTHUMBERLAND

A SHELL GUIDE

A SHELL GUIDE

NORTHUMBERLAND

by THOMAS SHARP

Carving above a window at Capheaton Hall

LONDON FABER & FABER

First published in 1937
by Faber and Faber Limited
24 Russell Square London WC1
Second edition 1954
Third edition 1969
Printed in Great Britain by
W. S. Cowell Ltd, Ipswich

SBN 571 04677 0

While the author is here expressing his personal views,
Shell-Mex and B.P. is pleased to be associated
with his book

ILLUSTRATIONS

The choice of illustrations in this book
has been the responsibility of the editor

PREFATORY NOTE

The Shell Guide to Northumberland and Durham was first published in 1937. A much extended and rewritten Guide limited to Northumberland was published in 1954. This new edition of that Guide is again much extended and rewritten, and is almost entirely newly illustrated.

All guide-books are indebted to other books for some of their information. This one shares the common indebtedness. Among other books from which information has occasionally been drawn are—for the description of the Roman Wall, Collingwood Bruce's *Handbook*, edited by Sir Ian Richmond; for the Gazetteer, C. L. S. Linnell's *Northumberland*; Sidney Moorhouse's *Companion to Northumberland*; and, for dates and ascriptions of buildings, Nicholas Pevsner's *Northumberland* in his "Buildings of England" series. Thanks are due to Oriel Studios for photographs by Ursula Clark which appeared in *Historic Architecture of Newcastle-upon-Tyne* (edited by Bruce Allsopp).

1969   T.S.

The Percy Lion, Alnwick

THE FACE OF NORTHUMBERLAND

The Countryside

Geology and the history of agricultural development are rather frightening subjects, especially to him who wishes both to run and to read, as readers of guide-books generally want to. They are no doubt subjects for specialists. Nevertheless, if we want to appreciate the individuality of any countryside that we are going to look at, it is worth while to realize something of these matters even before we begin to look about, for we may then get a rough idea of what to expect.

The principle of it is something like this. The appearance of any countryside is determined in two ways: by what man has inherited in the chaos of its created form, and what he has done with that heritage. He has inherited a complex structure of rocks (a geological formation) already moulded into hills and valleys whose configuration he can do little to alter. Over these are laid soils of differing natures. These soils place certain limits upon what he can grow in order to live. Similarly he has to take as he gets it that other natural phenomenon which influences his activities, the weather. But given these materials and limitations, he is free to do as he likes with his landscape; and although he cannot actually mould and shape it, he is always, consciously or unconsciously, adapting and decorating it to suit his own needs. Without irreverence we may perhaps put it in this way: the countryside is the fabric of one *Great Creator* or *Accident* (according to which belief you incline), adapted by generations of small human creators for their own purposes.

For a broad description, the natural face of Northumberland may be said to comprise four fairly distinct forms. First there is the flat featureless triangle of the south-east corner where the coal measures lie. The narrow coastal plain which stretches most of the way up to Berwick, eastwards of the Great North Road, is a continuation of this, for the main part without the underlying coal. Then there is a middle belt, running from about Warkworth south-westwards to the North Tyne at about Chollerford, north of Hexham, for the most part upland country, rather bare, with wide windy fields and few small hedgerow trees—and those mostly late-leafing ash, so that this belt can sometimes look rather stubbornly wintry even up to the first weeks of June. Beyond that, northwards and westwards, stretching over the greater part of the county, is the hill-and-valley Cheviot country which contains the essence of what one thinks of as individually Northumbrian. And south of it, on the other side of the Tyne Gap, is the considerable knob of hill-and-valley country that is different again—Pennine rather than Cheviot country in character.

That is the unalterable background of the Northumbrian landscape. What superficial pattern have men put upon it? Well, in the south-east corner some of their decorations are of a type that is unpleasant to most people. On the one hand, the bleakness of this level coastal strip and the character of the land have prevented the addition of many natural decorative features. Except in the sheltered glens of the rivers *Blyth* and *Wansbeck* there are not many trees there, and the hedges are scraggy. But if men have not been able to do much with the surface, the coal measures have given them plenty to do under it; and to the natural bleakness of their district they

BLYTH Sands
Coquetdale near HEPPLE
Border landscape near CARHAM

Monks House: by the dunes south of BAMBURGH
BAMBURGH Castle
SEAHOUSES Harbour

have added an artificial bleakness in features such as pit heaps. This is a landscape which neither man nor the Great Accident has made very attractive.

If you are a stranger to the county, and arrive at this part first, passing along the western edge of it on the Great North Road from *Newcastle*, you will not, it is to be hoped, regard this district as typical of Northumberland. It is really only a small corner of it, and you will find the rest of the county very different.

Take first the sea coast. This for the greater part is bordered by long stretches of blown sand pitched up, in many places, into high sandhills. Even where there is no blown sand the coast for most of its length is fringed with fine tide-washed sands, and is broken frequently into bays, many of them of that desirable smallness that brings out beauty of line and gives a comfortable intimacy of scale. Generally the coast-line is low. There are not a great many cliffs, but what there are are fine—mostly sheer iron-hard dolerite crags terminating the Whin Sill where it slashes in thin lines across the county. There are impressive examples of these at *Dunstanburgh* and *Bamburgh*, each of them crowned by a castle. Some of the islands too (of which Northumberland has more than an average share), are dolerite, and several have lighthouses on them, so that a seaward view on this coast nearly always has some special feature to engage attention. Add to this that the coast is long (about 70 miles), and that most parts of it are sufficiently far from large centres of population not yet to have been over-developed (though there are parts enough that are wrecked by shacks and caravans), and you will realize that in its sea-board Northumberland has a feature from which there is a good deal of pleasure to be got.

Back from the coast, the land rises steadily to the uplands and the hills. In almost every part of the county one is conscious of the hills. They crown most north-western and western prospects, rising and falling against the sky line. It is not always the main bulk of the Cheviots that does

so. In the middle part of the county the *Simon-sides* intervene with their fine wave-like outline. Back a little from the northern coast, the low ranges of the *Kyloe Hills* and the *Belford* and *Chatton Moors*, though they are of no great height, diversify the scene and provide wide seaward and landward views.

In the valleys the rivers are almost always edged or embowered, after their first infant miles, in woods. The *North* and *South Tynes* are really noble streams, carrying a much greater bulk of water than any of the others, except the *Tweed*, which, though it borders the county for some 17 or 18 miles and is wholly within it for another four or five, is in reality a Scottish river. But though the *Coquet*, the *Till*, the *Wansbeck* and the *Blyth* are somewhat smaller in volume, they are none the less full of character, as are the lesser streams, the *Aln*, the *Breamish*, the two *Allens*, *Warksburn*, *Harthope Burn* and many others.

The hills among which these rivers rise and run have a striking character. For the most part the Cheviots are very different from the long whale-backed fells of the Pennines. They have more separate summits. And though none of them is sufficiently high or sufficiently rugged to be called a mountain, *The Cheviot* itself being only 2,676 feet high and the least characteristic of them all, they make a far bumpier panorama than moorland country generally does.

In fact they are not moorland hills in the ordinary sense, except for those, south of the Tyne Gap, which are physically part of the genuine Pennine mass. There are, of course, many stretches of whale-backed country: but even these have a character of their own. The difference probably lies in vegetation as much as in outline, for these hills are not all covered with rough fell grass and heather as most Pennine country is. Most of them carry smoother, finer bent-grass which in sun and cloud-shadow, and in wind, produces a surprisingly varied range of tone in the scene. And, wild and lonely as they

College Burn, KIRKNEWTON
WESTNEWTON
ALWINTON

FARNE ISLANDS

are, they are curiously more humanized, as well as more diversified, than moorland country generally is; for besides the remote and solitary shieling or shepherd's cottage or farmhouse that one can come across in unexpected places, the sense of human impropriation is established by the wide-scattered and geometric-shaped plantations which occasionally stand out on the hillsides in all but the bleakest parts. And the scenery they make is extraordinarily varied. It is a scenery of great wind-swept, rain-washed, sun-splashed, cloud-dappled panoramas. There is nothing monotonous about these Northumberland Cheviots. They are full of change, contrast, variation. And because of this they seem somehow less savage, less sterile than ordinary fell and moorland country, somehow more friendly to the human spirit: and (in most weathers, at least) they seem to have an invigorating rather than an oppressive quality. To speak of them in this way is not to reduce their stature. Cheviot country is immensely wide, wild and lonely. But it is also strongly individual and very varied. And in that it is additionally attractive.

The difference between this Cheviot country and that south of the Tyne Gap adds to the county's variety. The Pennine country here has a strongly compact character. It is more broken, with steeper narrower dales between its close and roughly parallel ridges. Its tops are heather covered, and its trees in the lower dales are more dense. This, though less individually Northumbrian, is also very individual country.

To the natural individuality of these landscapes men have added another individuality in their own humanization of them. Hill country and lowland alike show Northumberland to be by far the most feudal county in England. Feudal is not too strong a word, and it is not suggested only by the survival of the medieval castles— though it *is* by the number of estate-villages and hamlets. If every castle had disappeared, the countryside would still proclaim this to be a county of great land-owners. Its landscape is not, of course, a feudal landscape. It would not be so humanized if it were. But in character it is definitely a land-owners' landscape.

It is strongly contrasted, for instance, with the neighbouring county of Durham. There, particularly in the middle and west, you have small fields divided by hedgerows or walls, with plenty of single-standing trees in them. That is the landscape of the small individual farmer. Northumberland is nothing like this. Nearly everywhere the fields are large, and there are not so many hedges and not many trees in them. The woods are in the parklands of the great houses, or lining the roads approaching them, in the river valleys, or are dotted about in square or round plantations on isolated knolls or on the broader hillsides. This landowners' countryside is seen particularly well in the valleys of the two Tynes (and is shown in the country behind the *Wall* in the photograph on pages 36–37 of this book); but it is a very marked feature everywhere, and is one of the most striking individual characteristics of Northumberland.

It can all be explained, of course, in the history of the county. All this countryside was frontier territory long after the rest of England was settled and peaceful. It was not merely the battle ground between the two crowns of England and Scotland: it was also a debatable land subject to raiding that involved pillage and murder and the carrying off of horses and cattle by rival families and clans on both sides of the border. Against this war and raiding the powerful families lived in their great castles, and the lesser gentry in their peel towers; but the smaller folk were less protected, and their huts were subject to being burnt as a matter of course in any hostilities, while they themselves and their cattle took to the woods or found shelter in a nearby peel.* An official report of 1570 relating to Bywell (see Gazetteer, p. 68) describes how, even at that late date, the country right down to the main Tyne valley (and within less than fifteen miles of Newcastle itself) was still subject to ravaging and

* For the architectural results of this see "The Fortified Frontier" (pp. 33–46).

The North Tyne
The Coquet

pillaging by the county's own "moss-troopers" from the wild areas of Tynedale and Redesdale. The union of their crowns in 1603 ended the border fighting between the two countries, but even after the formal Act of Union, in the early years of the eighteenth century, raiding was not unknown; and there was still a County Keeper who drew the then huge salary of £500 a year in return for making good the value of stolen cattle.

It was not, indeed, until well into the eighteenth century that most of the county was brought into settled agricultural use. Then the making of roads, the draining of moorland farms, the planting of woods, the enclosure of the waste, began to shape the face of the countryside to the large-scale pattern we see today. It was not only the imposition of order on lawlessness that made this possible. It was also the prosperity of the developing industries of Newcastle and the south-east corner of the county. Tyneside money made in coal and the mercantile trade was invested in the land. Political events brought about changes in ownership, especially through the ousting of some of the old families who had supported the Stuart cause, and the acquisition of their estates by newer industrial families. "Newcomers brought with them their industrial wealth and poured it into the estates they had bought to increase the rent of their farms, the prosperity of their tenants and the amenity of their country houses."* Even so, as late as the 1770s, Arthur Young could report that "there are at least 600,000 acres waste in the single county of Northumberland"—which meant at least half the total area of the county.

Still, by 1794, it could be reported that "plantations on an extensive scale are rising in every part of the county": and it was in these years in the eighteenth century, and later in the early nineteenth, that Northumberland began to get its present aspect. It was a period when Englishmen everywhere were seized by a great enthusiasm for beautifying their countryside. In other districts, where ownerships were on a small scale, trees were planted mostly in the hedgerows, because there was no other room to spare. But here the great landowners concentrated on parks and woods, without troubling much about hedgerow planting; and it was they who gave much of Northumberland its present scenic pattern—which is why in many parts it shows plainly, even today, its semi-feudal social state, still under the domination of the great house.

The changes that took place after the pacification of the debatable lands were not, of course, primarily aesthetic ones. They arose out of changes in rural economy. And in this, in at least two examples, Northumberland pioneered developments which had their effect not only within the county but much farther afield.

One of these had an altogether unintended and unexpected effect. It was Northumberland (Cheviot) sheep that were the innocent instruments that led to the depopulation of the Scottish glens. The Cheviot (according to John Prebble, the historian of *The Highland Clearances*) "was almost man-made . . . Once known as the Long Hill sheep, a distinct and hardy race of animals had grazed there (in the Cheviots) for six centuries. . . . By the middle of the eighteenth century they were still lank and gibbety, long-necked and thin at the shoulders. It was a Cheviot farmer called Robson who began to turn them into the great beast that would become the four-footed clansmen of the Highlands." The native sheep of the Highlands were both poorer in wool and meat and unadapted to winter exposure on high ground. The Cheviot was a winner in all respects. His fame spread until it became almost an hysteria among the great landowners of the Highlands to have their hills and croftlands covered by Cheviots. And as they were brought in in their thousands the crofters in the glens were thrust out on to the sea in ship-loads bound for America—an altogether unintended and tragic revenge from Northumberland against the Scots (though they had been Lowlanders) who had given them so many centuries of trouble on their border.

---

* Trevelyan: *English Social History*.

18

The other Northumbrian development in rural economy had a universally beneficent rather than a calamitous (though distantly located) effect. This was the great improvement in the milk-yield of the Shorthorn. That breed of cattle had been first developed in the neighbouring county by Charles Colling at a farm near Darlington. From the Durham Ox, bred by Colling in the 1780s, have sprung all the Shorthorns of the world. But the early animals were bred for beef; and it was Thomas Bates, at Halton in the Tyne valley (and later at Kirklevington in the North Riding) who somewhat later on bred the branch that became the most popular of all dairy cows.

Sheep and cattle continue to be the basis of the county's rural economy. Northumberland is generally thought of among farmers as chiefly beef-and-sheep-raising country. And so it still is. The coastal strip around Belford and Bamburgh, especially, is considered by many to be the richest fattening ground in the country. But even in the dairying country of the Tyne valley and the coastal strip south of Alnwick the farms tend to be large. Over most of the rest of the county they can be very large indeed. The sheep farms of the hills can indeed be enormous by English standards. There is one which runs to some 9,500 acres—the largest farm in the country. But the lowland farms, too, have unusually great acreage, especially those in the cattle-sheep-and-barley country of the northern half of the county, between Tweedside and Alnwick. There, in highly-mechanized mixed farming, holdings of 1,000 acres are quite common (there are some 65 farms of that size) and 750 acres is not considered a big size for a farm.

All this is reflected in the face of the land. It is, today, a continuation and a maturing of the landscape that was begun mainly in the eighteenth and early nineteenth centuries. But as well as the continuance of these old forms and appearances there is now taking place in some parts of the county's hill country an agronomic revolution as dramatic in its scenic effects as was that earlier

The Allen, near Staward Peel. See HAYDON BRIDGE

revolution itself. The new revolution is in the development of the great forests that are being planted by the Forestry Commission, acting as the agent of Government. An area of some two hundred and more square miles of Cheviot country is being quite transformed—transformed beyond all recognition from grassy sheep walk into vast forest of (mainly) Sitka and Norway spruce. In the country westward of *Simonburn* and *Wark*, or into the valley of the North Tyne northwards from *Bellingham*, or up Redesdale along the Jedburgh road from *Rochester*, there are now great panoramas of forest, some parts straight-lined with little trees only recently planted on the upturned turves of drainage furrows that have been cut by tractor-plough, others already thick and massive from the first plantings of more than forty years ago.

As a traveller you may or may not like what you see there. Most of us who have loved these grassy hills with their soft, many-tinted, cloud-shadowed outlines, their sense of wide, unrestricted freedom, their clean free air, cannot but regret the beauty that has gone, But when these forests have matured they too will have some beauty of their own. And in any event, the case for the change is incontestable. In the planting that is now going forward much hardly-used land is being brought into enormously increased productivity for human benefit. Where before, as sheep walk, it employed one man to approximately every 500 acres, as maturing forest it will employ twenty times as many; and the cash value of the new crops will be many times that of the old. And that, indeed, is how this kind of change must be regarded in all areas of semi-waste lands such as these (but not in areas of special scenic and recreational value like the Lake District). For trees are a crop as corn and cattle and sheep and potatoes are: and in an over-populated country like England every acre needs to be brought to its greatest usefulness.

That then is the face of rural Northumberland. Without a doubt it is far and away the quietest large tract in England. Think for a moment of the fact that, even including Tyneside (one of the most densely populated areas in the country),

21

Northumberland is still relatively one of our least populous counties. If you remember that the industrial area carries something like 80 per cent of the total population of the county (some 850,000) and is less than a tenth of the whole (and it is the fifth largest county in the country, covering some 20,000 square miles), then you will have some idea how quiet the rest is. It is a countryside of great peace and solitude. In all this wide county outside the industrial corner, there are just over half a dozen small towns, and not many more than a dozen substantial villages. Even in the lowland parts you can travel for miles among trees and fields and see only a hamlet or two and a few dozen farm-houses, and meet only half a dozen other cars. It is the perfect county for ambling in, just driving quietly along and running down a side road every now and then to discover some unfrequented place. Unexpectedly enough these wide, lonely, pastoral districts are crossed by an amazingly intricate net-work of roads, and these still more unexpectedly, are kept in excellent condition (though unfortunately, frequently ill-signed). There are hundreds of little side-roads that go for miles without passing a cottage and yet are maintained with a smooth tarred surface—a surface, sometimes, as on some of the main roads, too, which the road-makers have regrettably given a strong red finish that seems to bring an alien reminder of industrial urban-ness into the countryside. Sometimes, of course, you will get on to a dead-end road, or on to a stretch where you may have to get out and open a gate or two. But these little roads are always worth trying; they can land you into enchanting or exciting places, and even if they don't they can be charming in themselves; and driving along them, meeting hardly a soul, you may almost think they have been made for your special benefit. It would be invidious to

South Tyne Valley near KNARESDALE

mention even a few of these roads to the exclusion of others; and to make a complete list would be too great a task.* But there are sufficient of them to keep you busy for a long time, and in all that time you will be constantly rewarded. And when you have truly felt the spirit of Northumberland, all this countryside will draw you back again and again, for its quietness has a strange appeal in these hurried and difficult years that we are passing through.

As for those who prefer walking instead of, or together with, motoring, here again the county offers riches. In the lowland country there is a multitude of field paths; and the hills are free (except when, above Otterburn, the military are firing their guns). Even in the forests the Forestry Commission is providing new footpaths of a kind that are uncommon in England. And there are two special features, the Northumberland National Park and the Pennine Way, that protect the landscape and provide access to it.

The National Park takes in a great area of the hill-country between Wooler in the north and the Roman Wall towards Housesteads in the south. It is some 40 miles long, 5 miles at its narrowest and 16 miles at its greatest width: and the Pennine Way runs through its total length as well, of course, as far beyond. The longest footpath in Britain (it is 250 miles long), there are altogether some 60 miles of it in Northumberland. It enters the county on its southern boundary a mile or two north of Alston, follows the South Tyne valley and the line of the old Roman road, the Maiden Way, to Greenhead; then travels along the Wall at one of its most impressive sections over the Nine Nicks of Thirlwall, Whinshields, and the heights above Crag Lough, almost to Housesteads, where it enters the National Park. There it goes between Greenlee Lough and Broomlee Lough, across the moors and through Wark Forest, to Bellingham: and from there to Byrness by Hareshaw Linn and Lord's Shaw

* Unfortunately a great many of these side-roads cannot be shown on the comparatively small-scale map which is all that can be included in a book like this. But with half-inch scale maps you can safely go along virtually every road that is marked there with a double line, and, indeed, some that are not.

(1,167 feet), passing by Rooken Cairn and over Blackwool Law. Then from Byrness it takes the longest and toughest stage of the whole 250 miles, the lonely 27-mile stretch to the Border and Kirk Yetholm, across almost totally uninhabited country which must be walked in one day—over Raven's Knowe (1,729 feet) to the Roman camps at Chew Green, then up and down right along the Border Fence, over Brownhart (1,664), Greystone Brae (1,512), Blackhall (1,573), Rushy Fell (1,580), Lamb Hill (1,676), Beefstand (1,842), Mozie Law (1,812), and Windy Rigg to Windy Gyle (1,963); then by Cock Law, King's Seat (1,784) and Crookedsyke Head to Auchope Cairn (2,382), and along the ridge to the Schil (1,965) and Black Hag, where it passes into Scotland and travels three miles or so down the Halterburn to Kirk Yetholm (the really energetic traveller being able to divert himself partway by the tiresome climb to the 2,676 foot top of the Cheviot, a horizontal mile on from Auchope Cairn, if he wishes to do so).

The Industrial Area

If the face of the great rural expanses of the county is wide and open and strikingly individual, that of the south-eastern industrial corner of it is very different not merely in character but also in quality. Flat and featureless, it could never have been more than somewhat bleak countryside even before it became industrialized. Now it is for the most part sombre as well.

It was, of course, the second half of the nineteenth century that produced most of the damage, though the twentieth century has done little to redeem it, and has indeed contributed a lot of its own. Before that, before the individual places were swamped by a torrent of development which ran them together in a mass of buildings broken only occasionally by waste areas and sad corrupted fields—before the full onset of large-scale industrialization, it was merely a gradually thickening scatter of villages concerned for the main part with the exploitation of coal—its mining, its transportation, its use in industries that depended upon it. The history of

Burradon Colliery, KILLINGWORTH

the area's economy may be briefly summed up in that one word COAL. Coal was the basis of all that followed—the development of the mercantile trade, shipbuilding, iron and steel manufacture, railways, engineering (and, as we have seen, the humanizing of the landscape in the rest of the county too).

The Romans won coal by surface mining. And it was for surface mining that the citizens of Newcastle were granted a charter in 1239, and the abbots of Newminster and others in the same century. By the time of Elizabeth pits were getting deeper and Northumberland "sea-coal" (so-called because it was transported by sea) was in general use not only in London and its surrounding areas but in other coastal and riverside places. In 1578 it was reported that, in the south, various trades "have long since altered their furnaces and fiery places and turned the same into the use and burning of sea-coal"— all of it from Tyneside (Durham coal being also transported from there). The port of Newcastle was built and lived on the export of coal, three-quarters of which went to London.

Directly connected with this was the development of shipping and the breeding of a tough race of seafarers. The coal was borne from the river banks to the carrying ships ("colliers") by the smaller boats or "keels" celebrated in the famous Tyneside song. For centuries the colliers bore the coal down to London and elsewhere—as they still do today. Even in Elizabethan times it could be said that these colliers (together with the fishing boats of Devon and Cornwall) were the "chief nurseries of English seamen". And later up to the advent of steam in the middle of the nineteenth century it could still be said that "the two great nurseries for foremast hands were the colliers and the coasters. . . . A man who could boast that he had served his time on a Geordie collier was considered to be true-blue—for there was no harder training in the whole wide world."*

From pit and collier sprang the beginning of railways. From the beginning of the 1600s, wooden rails were used on Tyneside to run the trucks of coal down to the river for loading the keels—and in the early 1700s no less than 20,000 horses were employed in the transport of coal in the environs of Newcastle alone. It was for the transport of coal from Wylam and other collieries that William Hedley and Timothy Hackworth developed the first true railway engine *Puffing Billy* (now in the Science Museum at Kensington) and George Stephenson about the same time (1814) developed his *Blucher* for carrying the coal from Killingworth colliery, a beginning which led to the building, on Tyneside, ten years later, of *Locomotion No. 1* (now at Darlington railway station) for the first passenger railway between Darlington and Stockton: and later, in 1830, the building by his son Robert, of the *Rocket*—probably the most famous engine ever built, and a proud display in the Kensington Science Museum since as long ago as 1862. So with all this and the great developments which followed, Tyneside may properly be said to be the birthplace of all the railways of the world.

And from coal, colliers and railway engines sprang modern shipbuilding and other forms of engineering and mechanical invention (the genius of the county seems to be far more in invention and its application—the invention of animals as well as machines—than in any of the arts). In the High Level Bridge at Newcastle, Robert Stephenson designed the first large bridge built of cast-iron. Parsons invented the first steam turbine here; and the first turbine-driven ship, the *Turbinia*, can be seen at the Municipal Museum of Science and Industry in the Exhibition Park of the Town Moor at Newcastle (along with some thousands of other exhibits of the county's invention and productiveness). Here

Armstrong developed his hydraulic engines and cranes and built up the enormous engineering undertaking that produced the various armaments he invented. Here the first dynamo was made: here Swan invented the electric bulb: and so on and so on.

It was on all this and much more (glass manufacture, chemical production etc. etc.) that this great industrial corner of Northumberland developed and flourished. It was all this that produced the grime, the wastelands, the urban disorder that characterizes Tyneside, as it does all other areas of nineteenth-century heavy industry. It is a sad thought that the places where splendid, impressive, sleek, even beautiful objects were produced—the foundries, the great workshops and the rest—and the places where the people who produced them lived, were and are themselves so abjectly unsplendid, so sordid, so disordered and mean. But such was the case everywhere in the nineteenth century and the early decades of this: and in this respect especially Tyneside shares the common heritage.

In seeing, or perhaps hurriedly passing through this part of the county, there is perhaps some consolation to be found in the thought that things should be better in the future. Today Tyneside is becoming less dependent on coal and ships and heavy industry (though even in 1964 over 46 per cent of Britain's total shipbuilding was under construction here). Now its industry is becoming much more diversified with lighter and cleaner manufacture, and its buildings and surroundings more presentable and more worthy of the things they produce and the people who produce them. Perhaps some day (but it will take a long time) even this part of the county will be made seemly and worthy again.

Towns, Villages, Buildings

The great attraction of Northumberland is its countryside. There is not much to say about its buildings by way of general introduction—except to give a warning not to expect too much. There are, of course, many noble buildings; there

* Basil Lubbock in *Early Victorian England 1830–65*.

The High Level Bridge, NEWCASTLE-UPON-TYNE 1849

are a great many that are fine or of some special interest, as well as great numbers that are decent and fitting and even handsome in an everyday kind of way. But they make few notable collective effects, except in the one or two small old towns, in Berwick especially, and in Alnwick, Warkworth, Hexham and Allendale Town; and, of course, in the distinguished central part of Newcastle.

The traditional building material everywhere in the county (and probably more extensively than in any other county) is sandstone—sandstone of a buff or dun colouring, much of which has weathered greyly in country places and darkly in the towns. (There has, of course, been a great deal of brick building in the later urban areas.) Sandstone slabs are also the traditional roofing material. These materials have produced some austerity of appearance in the frequent places where they are used together. But, as is the case along many other parts of the East Coast, there is also a lot of old roofing in red or brown-red pantiles on the more modest kinds of buildings; and these, where they occur, though they are "foreign" to the stone below them, sit very harmoniously upon it and give a glow of warmth and colour that in old groupings can

Quay Walls, BERWICK-ON-TWEED
Grey Street, NEWCASTLE-UPON-TYNE

create lively and indeed charming effects—such, for instance, as those made by the climbing roofs of Berwick when seen from across the Tweed. These pantiles are truly foreign, even though they have long been accepted as very happily characteristic of the districts where they occur, for it is said that they owe their presence here to being used as ballast in colliers returning empty after delivering the county's coal to Holland and the neighbouring parts of the Continent. This would account for their use in the coastal towns and villages, but it is, perhaps, surprising that they should have travelled so much farther afield than that, indeed right up into the western hills, where they can be seen in places like Harbottle.

These pantiled roofs on stone walls still exist in some of the older parts of the industrial section of the county. But they can do little to enliven the general effect there. As has just been indicated, the great "conurbation" that stretches practically uninterruptedly for a dozen miles and more along the Tyne, and, more brokenly, up the coast for another dozen, is grim and sordid in its worst parts and dreary and petty in all but its best. Hundreds of thousands of people live there in the long streets of the mining villages and the industrial towns. These places are home, however drab they may be; so they are enormously important to all those who live in them. But a guide-book for tourists should be honest and not given to a blind or over-tolerant local patriotism; and honesty compels one not merely to avoid particularizing these places here, but to say that no one could be advised to visit them unless they had need to. For this reason almost all these scores of towns, half-towns and villages in the south-eastern industrial triangle are omitted from the Gazetteer in this book—for there is nothing at all, or at least nothing that is good, so far as their looks are concerned, that one can say about them.

A special note of acknowledgement should perhaps be added. The later architectural history of Northumberland, in its larger buildings, is dominated, in a way probably unparalleled in any other county, by one name that occurs time after time in the ascription of the buildings of the

nineteenth century. John Dobson (1787–1865) must have had a practice of quite inordinate size, for besides designing central Newcastle for Richard Grainger (to say nothing of the noble Central Station there) he was over a long period engaged on newly building, rebuilding or restoring castles, dozens of country mansions, scores of churches and some bridges, as well as all manner of other buildings all over the county. Though his name is not much recorded in histories of English architecture, he was generally (though by no means always) a good architect, and sometimes a very good one. And the county should be grateful to his memory for it.

Miscellany

Speech Northumberland speech (or "twang" as it is called locally) may be a puzzle to visitors, and difficult at first for unaccustomed ears to catch. The most distinctive features about it are its speed and its lilt (each sentence ending several notes higher than it began), and its pronunciation of the letter *r*—the *burr*—by what has been described as "a rough vibration of the soft palate or pharynx". In the south of the county especially (the speech in the north and the west tends to be softer, though with much the same characteristics), there is also a good deal of duplication of vowel sounds so that, to give an example, one of the lines of the song "Geordie haud (hold) the Bairn" goes—

So Geordie *teuk* the bairn, tho' sair *agyen* hes will

for—

So Geordie took the bairn, tho' sore against his will.

There are a lot of dialect words and some older-English survivals—*gotten, yonder, thou, ye* and others. And numbers of corrupted foreign words; Scandinavian ones, perhaps surviving from earlier times or perhaps from the presence of the ports; some French derivations that are also common on the other side of the Border ("dinna *fash* yersel", don't trouble yourself, *fash* being a corruption and change of meaning from *facher*, to anger) —and could "*nettie*", the

BLYTH Harbour. The coal staithe is of a common type on this coast

curious common word for privy, somehow have got up here from the Italian *gabinetto*?

There are also, of course, idiomatic turns of speech. Thus 'Ye're looken *shabby* the day, Mrs Fenwick" wouldn't refer to her clothes, but to the lady's health: a day of poorish weather is apt to be "plain": and so on.

Place Names   There are some curious and expressive place names for farms, like Blinkbonny, Blawearie, Skirlnaked, Coldcotes, Bleakhope, Carrycoats, Wae's me, Farglow and Hope Alone; and for hills, like Bloodybush Edge, Beefstand, Cushat Law, High Cantle, High-spoon and Oh Me Edge.

Music   Most of the songs commonly sung as peculiarly Tyneside, including *Blaydon Races*, are merely Victorian music hall songs. But there are some beautiful older ones, including *The Water of Tyne*, *Blow the Wind Southerly*, *Captain Bover*, and of course *The Keel Row*. Many of the older Border ballads, though they are fine as poetry, are not really very singable as they are set to the music of the Northumbrian

bag-pipes—of which, incidentally, there are two kinds, the large or "half-long", for outdoor playing and the "small pipes" for indoor—both blown by bellows, not by the mouth.

Food   There are one or two local dishes, but they are nothing much to make a song about. *Singing Hinnies* are nice—hot buttered girdle cakes. *Pot-pie* and *Leek pudding* are food for hungry workers—the first is boiled in a pudding basin and is like steak-and-kidney pudding but with potatoes in it and a lot of rich gravy: the second is whole leeks in a long suet roll. *Spice-cake* is dark and rich and heavy with fruit. *Yule-doos* (or dolls) are eaten at Christmas—and are rather like a hot-cross bun, but with two currants for eyes and arms crossed in a lighter dough—clearly the Christ-child figure. And *carlings*, a kind of brown pea, are eaten on the second Sunday before Easter (the calendar being Tid, Mid, Miserae, Carling, Palm, Paste-egg Day) in celebration, tradition has it, of their being landed in a cargo on that day to relieve a siege of Newcastle.

THE FORTIFIED FRONTIER

Even today, much of the scenery of Northumberland has a frontier feeling. The rolling range of the Cheviots, crossed in a distance of nearly fifty miles by only three paved roads, still keeps the character of a Debatable Land which it historically had. Most of its old buildings, even some of its churches, have the appearance of outposts. The "theme song" of the county is fortification. It was begun in the scores of fortified places, some of them of great size, with which the early peoples sprinkled the hill-tops. It was repeated in the magnificent system of defence which the Romans centred on their great Wall that stretched from sea to sea. It was continued again in the British camps which were modelled on those that the Romans had made. It was reiterated through several hundred years of building medieval castles, peel towers, fortified manorhouses and rectories. It was finally given expression in the Military Road for which General Wade plundered and largely ruined the earlier Roman defensive system, which had stood for sixteen hundred years. Today, when the natives of Scotland exercise a more peaceful form of penetration, the theme song has dimmed away to a ghostly echo, but snatches of it may still be caught by whoever drives for an hour or so in this now most peaceful countryside.

British Camps

The early fortified villages and camps are so numerous, and so remotely situated on hill-tops far from roads or tracks, and, indeed, often enough with so little to show to the inexpert eye, that no one but the most enthusiastic specialist is likely to go to the pains of visiting many of them. The great camp on the top of *Yeavering Bell*, however, is readily accessible, and very well worth a visit. It takes in the whole summit of the hill, and was once enclosed by a vast wall of

'Cup and ring' markings, ROWTING Linn, DODDINGTON

loose stones. A few courses of this wall are still in position; and the rest are now scattered below the crest; but the general circuit of the walls, the positions of their gateways, of fortification trenches and hut circles, can still be traced even by those untrained in spotting antiquities.

Another fortified place, this one enclosed by two ramparts and also exhibiting hut circles, is at *Greaves Ash*, near Linhope, on the way from Ingram. But, indeed, there are innumerable examples. A glance at the one-inch ordnance map will show them especially thick, on every little summit almost, on the eastern foothills of the Cheviots, between *Kirknewton* and *Harbottle*. There are dozens, too, outside this particular stretch, and among these the camps at *Dod Law* and *Rowting Lynn* (near both of which there are also examples of the mysterious rock tracings commonly called "cup-and-ring markings") and others near Otterburn (such as *Green Chesters*) may be taken as typical.

The Roman Wall

Of the Roman Wall so much has been written that it is not necessary to describe it in any great detail here. The reader who wishes may study the known details in a dozen or more books,* and a host of scattered essays. Most of these books, however, do not sufficiently differentiate between the Wall as it was, and as it is. It is necessary, therefore, so as to avoid disappointment, to warn those who think to find something in the nature of the Great Wall of China, that over the greater part of its length Hadrian's Wall now consists of mere vestiges, that the most extensive

* By far the best account of the Wall is the authoritative *Handbook to the Roman Wall*, by J. Collingwood Bruce (10th edition, edited and brought up to date by Professor Sir Ian Richmond).

It might be worth recommending, as an introduction to the study of the Wall, a visit to the excellent little Wall Museum in Newcastle University–with models, relics, and a full size reconstruction of the Mithraic temple.

visible remains are nowhere *very* extensive, and that they do not easily thrust themselves upon one's notice, but have to be sought out with some little expenditure of time and energy. These facts accepted, an exploration of the Wall may provide a rich reward even to those who have no particularly marked bump of antiquarianism.

First of all, before briefly describing the Wall as it is, it is necessary to say a word or two about what it originally was. The Wall itself was but one element in a complicated defensive work running between Tyne and Solway. The whole work consisted of, first, a *ditch*, averaging about 27 feet broad and 9 feet deep, on the north side (except where the Wall ran along a position of strong natural defence like the crags near Housesteads): then a *berm*, a level space about 20 feet wide, to ensure a firm foundation for the wall and provide a track for the movement of troops: then the *wall*: then a military road about 20 feet wide: then, generally 60 or 80 yards back from the wall, the 40-yard wide earthwork known as the *vallum*, which was in itself quite a complicated affair, consisting of a central ditch

The Roman Wall and Crag Lough

20 feet wide and 10 feet deep, with, on each side, a level space 30 feet wide and then a mound 20 feet wide and about 6 feet high. Both the purpose and the date of the vallum (the purpose of the ditch in *front* of the wall is obvious) were for long uncertain, though it was thought that the vallum might have preceded the wall by as much as eighty years; but it has now been established that the two works are virtually contemporaneous and that the vallum was not a defence so much as a demarcation of the southern boundary of the military zone connected with the Wall, for the purpose of keeping out trespassers.

The Wall and its auxiliary works were constructed shortly after Hadrian became Roman Emperor in A.D. 117, during the time when

Aulus Platorius Nepos was Governor, about A.D. 122–126; and it was maintained and defended for 250 years, till 383, when disaster came upon Roman Britain. The whole, or at any rate by far the greater part, of the gigantic undertaking (seventy-four miles of Wall between Tyne and Solway) was completed in five years. Shortly after the beginning of the work, there was a change of plan. The original plan (which was partly carried out) was to build a wall 10 feet broad in Northumberland and a few miles beyond, where stone was plentiful, and a turf wall through most of Cumberland, where stone was more difficult to come by. This plan was

soon changed, however, and a stone wall was built over the whole length, to a width of 10 feet in some parts and 8 feet in others.

There is some uncertainty as to the exact height of the Wall. Bede, writing about 730, describes it as "eight feet in breadth, and twelve in height, in a straight line from east to west, as is still visible to beholders." In 1574 it is described at one place as "yet standing of the height of 16 fote for almost a quarter of a mile together". Camden, visiting the Wall in 1599, says: "within two furlongs of Carvoran on a pretty high hill the Wall is still standing, fifteen feet in height and nine in breadth." Altogether, it is now considered that the Wall was originally about 15 feet high at the rampart walk, with a parapet and merlons 5 feet on top of this, making a full height of about 20 feet in all. Even this height, however, was in effect much increased by the ditch which accompanied the Wall on its northern side.

The defence system was manned by patrolling garrisons housed in barracks on the Wall, and fighting garrisons housed immediately adjacent to it in forts. The garrison army consisted of about 5,500 cavalry and 13,000 infantry. Here, to quote from a recent leaflet, "at this farthest loneliest frontier of the Roman Empire, eighteen centuries ago" this army "ate, slept, grew corn, worshipped their gods, sweated the rheumatism from their limbs in hot steam baths—and kept a constant vigil against attacks from the wild northlands beyond the wall".

The patrol barracks, or *milecastles*, were placed regularly along the Wall at distances of a Roman mile (about 1,620 yards)—there were seventy-nine of them between Wallsend and Bowness in Cumberland—and they were each capable of accommodating up to fifty men. Every milecastle had a wide gateway on its north as well as its south side, for use as a sally-port. Between them, regularly spaced at distances of about 540 yards, there were twenty-foot-square *signalling-turrets*, two between every two milecastles.

The *forts* were not placed at regular intervals, but they were of more or less standard design

and type. There were nine of them in Northumberland and five in Cumberland. They had a regular pattern of streets, with military headquarters (and a chapel) at the centre, and the commandant's house and the massive buildings of the granaries (sufficiently big to hold a year's supply of grain) nearby, and, about these, rows of long, narrow buildings, mostly barracks but also stables, storehouses and workshops. Outside most forts lay a village, accommodating veterans and camp followers, and containing shops, taverns and the regimental bath house.

Besides these forts on the line of the Wall, there were a number of others, as well as camps, signal stations, and one or two places that were more nearly genuine towns than forts, situated on or near the main direct road, the *Stanegate*, that still exists, for very considerable stretches, in country lanes well south of Wall and vallum.

That briefly, is what the Wall *was* like. And now to come to some account of what the modern visitor may see. Begin at Newcastle and have *two* drivers in the car (for reasons which will be explained later). Taking the Hexham road you will get along as quickly as the traffic and the speed limit will allow, for there is nothing to detain you on this long arm of the Newcastle octopus, though in one or two places there are short stretches of a few courses of the Wall to be seen on the south side of the road.

At Heddon-on-the-Wall the main Hexham road bears left, but you will take the *Military Road* (straight ahead). Here signs of the Ditch, Wall and vallum appear; and then, beyond Harlow Hill the ditch becomes very plain, and for a long stretch is thickly grown with trees. A mile or so after the trees finish you come to the station Hunnum (Halton Chesters), where some important discoveries have been made, though there is not much to see. From here the road goes on again, with the ditch and vallum plain to see in most parts, till it drops down the long hill to Chollerford. Here the road veers away from the direct line: and, because its stones were spared in roadmaking, considerable remnants of the Wall have survived and been uncovered. These can now be glimpsed through the trees on the left,

Crindledikes Farm, south of HOUSESTEADS

and can be fully viewed, a continuous stretch several hundred yards long and four or five courses high, by turning to the left at the cross roads and going a short distance along the Hexham road.

Beyond Chollerford bridge, bearing left at the roundabout, the road passes the park of Chesters (see the Gazetteer for this, and the other main camps or forts). Here you should certainly stop by the Lodge on the left side of the road, for, passing into the park, you will see Cilurnum, one of the best exposed of all the stations on the Wall and, moreover, you will be in one of the richest scenes that Northumberland can show, a lovely park-like stretch of the North Tyne Valley, which you will remember in vivid contrast when you come to the frontier-like situation of Housesteads.

Leaving Chesters, the road climbs up the other side of the valley, and it is worth stopping towards the top to glance again at the backward view. In about a mile you may notice on the right of the road a cottage with a castellated eastern gable, built of fine square stones: they are Roman stones; and, indeed, if you have looked carefully, you may have noticed many such buildings as you have come along. Now the road drops a little, then rises on a sharp straight hill. This is Limestone Bank, and here, in the field on the right, stretches of the Wall are again to be seen standing four or five courses high.

After about another mile the road passes the site of the fort Procolita, where a Mithraic Temple has been excavated: then, about three miles farther on, at a dip a little beyond the small lake that is seen on the left, the road, the Wall, and the vallum all part company. The road keeps to the more level ground; the Wall strides on boldly, holding to the very crest of the fine wave-like hills which for the last few miles have brought a new and exciting feature into the landscape; and the vallum takes an easy line off the whinstone about half-way between the two. Here the two drivers should also part company, one to begin walking westwards, the other driving on for about five miles and then himself walking eastwards.*

Walking westward, one now sees the interest of both the Wall and the scenery mounting the whole time. At first there are mere vestiges of the Wall, a rough irregular mound here and there, with a few stones showing. Even the line is a little difficult to follow after passing the first cottage; but, by keeping on through the wood at the top of the rise alongside the boundary wall of Sewing Shields farmhouse (which is entirely built out of the stones of the Wall) you will eventually come on to more open land and will then go along the edge of the crags on the windy summit where the Wall itself once added a further 20 feet of height to the great natural defences. Here and for some distance there is a high modern field wall running along the real Wall's line, rising and falling with the hill-crests. Then some distance this side of *Housesteads*, you will come at last on appreciable remains of the Wall itself. Not, of course, the full Wall: only some four or five feet of it, built of fine square stones, running and rising away in the distance to the horizon: but at last it is indubitably THE WALL.

The interest of a mere wall, even a Roman wall, would be bound to flag after a mile or so were there nothing else to stimulate it. But here the interest is not only increased but is far surpassed by the interest of its surroundings. Up and down the wave-like hills the Wall goes. Mostly it is along the edge of high crags, but sometimes its line softens a little, and occasionally it passes through a wood. And far more inspiring than the details of its immediate path is the magnificent wide panorama of its setting. This is the genuine frontier country. To the north roll wide unenclosed almost treeless grassy uplands; not moors, nor yet fells, but low-rolling wastes of a very distinctive character, and of a most striking beauty. About these wastes are dotted a few sparse sheep farms which only seem to accentuate the frontier feeling. And three dark lonely loughs, one of which lies at the very foot of the wall-surmounted crags, complete the effect of remoteness and isolation.

Not that the country behind the Wall is rich in contrast to this bare edge of things: that, too, has a feeling of emptiness about its wide rolling fields. But there is just that difference; there *are* fields, man-made symbols of a settled civilization. And there are trees, too; not parkland or hedge-row trees, but great circular or rectangular plantations, which give a striking pattern in direct contrast to the bareness of the country on the other side.

All these things you will see as you walk the heights towards Housesteads fort. And you will see still more beyond Housesteads, for now the Wall is in splendid condition. There is still no great height to it, but you can walk along the top of it, on its turf-protective covering, and with only a little self-deception you may yourself feel some of the emotions that the Romans perhaps felt when they paced it eighteen hundred years ago.

So the Wall goes on, now at its best, up and down, sheer above the secret water of Crag Lough, through an occasional coppice as before. There are some rougher steeper pitches on the stretch beyond Housesteads, but they are no trouble to any ordinarily active person. In the clean clear air of these heights you will find an additional stimulant to activity. And by the time you reach your car you will not only have seen

* Let the arrangements be quite clear, or there will be some extra miles of uncertain walking. Here one driver, *A*, will get out to begin his five-mile walk, going through the fieldgate on the right of the road. The other driver, *B*, will drive on till he comes, at the scattered hamlet called *Once-Brewed*, to the first road leading north. Taking this side road for about half a mile, he will come to the Wall right on top of the hill. Here he will leave the car in the car-park nearby, lock it, and begin walking the Wall eastwards. He will meet *A* about half way (or, say, at *Housesteads*, where they can look at the fort together), and will hand over the key of the car. *A* will continue westwards, *B* eastwards, and *A* will eventually come to the car and will drive it eastwards, to where *B* will be waiting for him at the place where they originally parted company.

the finest stretch of this finest British monument of antiquity, you will also have done one of the grandest walks in the British Isles.

There is fine Wall-walking westwards from the Once-Brewed road, as well as eastwards; and there are places on the westward stretch where the two-driver trick can be done. In the eight miles by way of Bogle Hole and Thorny Doors to the Haltwhistle Burn, and then beyond that to the county boundary at Greenhead, there are some good stretches of the Wall to be seen, though in many places it has all but disappeared. And here again the setting is superb. The walk (which has been incorporated as part of the Pennine Way) is wind-blown and exhilarating, with immense views at 1,230-feet-high Whinshields (including, on a clear day, the distant Solway Firth and the Dumfriesshire and Kirkcudbrightshire hills), and with something like a wave-cresting progress over the Nine Nicks of Thirlwall, and always with the lonely frontier country on the north.

Whichever way you walk on this central dozen-mile stretch of the Roman Wall, you will be able to say, as Camden did in 1599, "Verily I have seene the tract of it over the high pitches and steepe descent of hilles, wonderfully rising and falling".

Castles

If you have to set yourself out to find the evidences of the Roman fortified frontier you cannot easily avoid seeing reminders of the medieval system of fortification. There are more castles to the mile, and more battle-sites, in Northumberland than in any other part of the British Isles. A catalogue of 1415 listed thirty-seven large castles and seventy-eight smaller ones. Another of 1541 listed, in only a part of the county, no less than one hundred and twenty castles of various types. Many of these buildings have, of course, completely vanished; many more are but a heap of stones on a knoll; but even today there are some sixty or seventy castles, large or small, inhabited or but ruined shells, scattered about the Northumberland countryside.

This may conjure up a vision of a ring of

WARKWORTH Castle
ALNWICK Castle
BELSAY Castle

fortresses silhouetted boldly on hill-tops against the sky-line. Actually it is nothing like so romantic as that. The castles are scattered, and though only the laziest traveller can avoid seeing a dozen or more, some of the others are not easy to find. The keepers of the border sought the valleys rather than the hill-tops. A strong site hidden from the invader, from whence you might issue for unexpected attack or whither you might retreat in times of trouble, was more useful in border warfare than advertising yourself on the heights. Add to this that the castles which have not gone to ruin have been adapted to a more domestic mode of life, and have often been surrounded by private parks and heavy woods, and you will not expect the too obviously romantic when you set out looking for a castle you may have read about in a border ballad.

It would be useless to try to describe all the castles here. Most of the more important ones are mentioned in the Gazetteer; and, anyhow, the interest of many people extends to their romantic associations as much as to their physical form, and for these details we have no room. Since, however, the term applies to a wide range of fortified buildings, from a vast ducal stronghold to a comparatively insignificant tower, it may be useful to give a few brief notes on the various types of castle.

The earliest type of medieval stronghold was the Norman motte-and-bailey, in which a strong natural position was strengthened by artificial means, the piling-up of an artificial mound, the steepening of hillsides, the cutting of ditches and building of ramparts. There is an excellent example of this at *Elsdon*. Later came the great rectangular keep such as is seen at *Newcastle* and *Norham*. In the fourteenth century a type was developed which consisted of a great area enclosed by strong walls and protected by a massive gatehouse, of which *Dunstanburgh* is an outstanding example. Another fourteenth-century type consisted of a rectangular courtyard with square

41

Union Bridge (1820), Loan End, HORNCLIFFE

defensive towers at the angles. *Chillingham* is a fine specimen of this kind. Still another fourteenth-century kind of castle is the great tower-house, somewhat in the nature of the earlier Norman keep, *Warkworth* being a splendid example of it.

In some of the larger castles, as for instance at *Alnwick*, these various types got mixed up, one type accreting on to another; and besides these well-marked classes of permanent defensive structure, there were many kinds of half-domestic, half-defensive smaller buildings, as well as some that must have been built only for refuge in case of necessity. These are mostly of the single-tower-house type, and they range considerably in size, from the large examples of *Langley* and *Haughton*, through the somewhat lesser ones at *Belsay* and *Chipchase*, to that small and varied class which may be loosely described as "peels" or "peles". They also range considerably in date, as from the thirteenth-century example at *Simonburn* to those of the late sixteenth century at *Doddington* and *Coupland*.

NORHAM Castle

Besides these again, there are other different types of fortified houses ranging from the fortified manor-house of *Aydon Castle* to the embattled rectories such as are to be seen at *Elsdon*, *Corbridge* and *Embleton*. And one must not neglect to mention the churches. In the last resort, these, too, were sometimes used as refuges, and for other quasi-military purposes. Thus the inhabitants of Warkworth took sanctuary in the parish church and were massacred there by William the Lion of Scotland in 1173, and the church burned over them. Thus also several churches are known to have been much damaged (as Durham Cathedral was damaged) by Scottish prisoners who were held captive in them. In some places, as at *Edlingham*, part of the church seems to have been definitely designed as a prison. And as final examples of the lawlessness of the Border which demanded all this fortification and perpetual watchfulness, we may cite marks on the pillars near the door in Elsdon church, which are said to be where men sharpened their swords when they were suddenly called out from prayer to battle.

The Whiteadder. Northumberland north of the Tweed

The Border Today

Today it is only in one or two places that you may experience very much of the special sensation that seems called for as you pass from one country into another. If the Tweed were the Border at Berwick, as it is sometimes mistakenly thought to be, then here one might be forgiven feeling something of the thrill of an Event as one passed over it, for it is a noble and formidable barrier. Actually one may enter Scotland from Berwick quite unawares in a number of places, by merely crossing an obscure ditch. It is the same on the six roads crossing from Carham, Sunnylaws, and Mindrum, in the country between the Tweed and the beginning of the Cheviots. Nothing more than a slight difference of road surface denotes the change here. The bridge crossings over the Tweed at *Union Bridge*, *Norham*, and *Coldstream* are definite enough: but it is the two hill crossings

that are most telling. That on the wild road at *Deadwater*, beyond the head of the North Tyne above Kielder, leaves no doubt that this is a frontier country, though the crossing itself is obscure. But it is perhaps only the pass at Carter Bar that gives a strong sense of an Event. Here signposts are provided telling what is happening to you; but you do not need this, for you are right at the top of the steep-sided divide, and you cannot but feel that the unusual-looking hills billowing away on the north-east are a barrier and a boundary of some importance: and for this the tourist, the writer of guide-books and the Scottish Nationalist should all feel appropriately thankful.

NORHAM
THE ROMAN WALL, near Housesteads
Fortified Vicarage at CORBRIDGE

46

GAZETTEER

The number after the place name indicates the square on the map where the place is to be found

Allendale Town (17). A good substantial little town among fine hill and valley scenery of Pennine character (it was over-harshly described in previous editions of this guide because of a ribbon of 1930 semis which trails out along the road towards Catton). The stone-built market-place, and the wide main street with its trees and greens have a very attractive character. There are one of two largish hotels, one, the Hotspur, with a pedimented doorway and miniscule three-storey stone bow-windows on either side. The nineteenth-century church is splendidly placed on a high wooded bank above the river. On a wall there, a sundial has the town's latitude and longitude (the town claims to be at the middle of Britain). A fire-station

on the hillside to the north-east has a tall tower which makes a prominent contributory feature to the landscape setting.

A curate here, Robert Patten, played a considerable part in the 1715 Jacobite rebellion, turned King's Evidence, and wrote a history of the affair.

There are great doings on New Year's Eve: a big bonfire at midnight; and fancy-dressed men marching about with pans of blazing tar on their heads.

Allenheads (17). A snugly-clustered hamlet on a piney enclave with the moors all round, at the head of East Allendale, a fine wide dale which changes as it gets higher and narrower from hedged to stone-walled country.

ALLENDALE TOWN
Shawhouses, below ALLENHEADS

Beyond the hamlet the road climbs stiffly over the county boundary into County Durham.

West Allendale, roughly parallel to East Allendale, with three miles of hill slopes between, is also a fine dale, deeply wooded in its lower part, wide and open above, where the road rises to 1,999 feet to cross the heights (and the county boundary) to join the road over Killhope, the second highest main-road pass in Britain. The two dales were centres of lead-mining and used to produce a seventh of all the lead in the kingdom. The scars of the old workings are almost all long since grown over; and

WARKWORTH (opposite)
Market Place, ALNWICK (below)

ALNMOUTH, *Alnwick's seaside*

they now give a curious character to certain parts of the district.

Alnham (8). A widely scattered hamlet at the foot of the hills. Once a place of more importance. A bare stone-roofed little church dating from about 1200, but much restored in the nineteenth century after long being ruinous. The vicarage a "vicar's peel", fortified like those at Corbridge, Elsdon and elsewhere. Foundations of a castle on a green mound. And little else besides.

Nearby are two early village sites; also Castlehill Camp, a large contour earthwork, 300 yards across; and another camp at High Knowes.

Alnmouth (pron. Alem'th) (9). Long an important grain port. Now a small and quiet seaside place. It makes a pleasant picture of river, sea and village from the coast road and the main railway line nearby. Though there is nothing specially distinguished in its buildings, it has fine sands, pleasant coast walks, good

fishing, two golf courses (one the third oldest in England); and no promenades.

To the north, overlooking the sea, is Beacon Hill Camp, a quadrangular earthwork. South of the river, on a steep grassy hill cut off from the town when the river changed its course, are the foundations of the Saxon church of St Waleric.

Alnwick (pron. Annick) (9). A splendidly-situated small town, full of character and interest. On market

ALNWICK. *The Percy Column*

The Barbican. Opposite: *The Lion Bridge*

days (Mondays and Fridays), and on Saturdays, it is crowded with people from all the villages, hamlets and lonely farmhouses for miles around. In the main streets one parks one's car at an exciting angle on sloping cobbles.

The Percy Lion, with its poker-like tail, dominates the town. At the top of a little knoll at the east entrance, by the railway station, it stands high on a fine column, designed by David Stephenson, and "erected, dedicated and inscribed by a grateful and united tenantry, 1814" (and sometimes known as "The Farmer's Folly", for, being built in recognition of the Duke of Northumberland's liberality

in remitting rents during a period of agricultural depression, it naturally made him think that his tenants weren't so badly off after all, so he put the rents up again). The lion is also on the bridge on the Berwick road, on the coat of arms of the Castle Barbican, and in other places.

All the main streets of the town are good, solid, stone-built, plainish but not over-severe, nicely diversified with a quiet northern unpretentiousness. Bailiffgate, a fine wide short street, between the church and the castle has these good plain buildings, and has pollarded limes growing among sloping cobbles. Clayport, Fenkle Street, Bondgate are all good streets. Narrowgate not only has good buildings but also a curving form which sustains the interest through varying views. And the

Percy Street, Percy Terrace, Lisburn Street neighbourhood of neat two-storeyed houses and villas of about 1830–40 has an ordered and restrained character that is pleasantly unified.

The fifteenth-century parish church (St Michael's), its strongly buttressed tower well situated above a steep bank overlooking the river, has splendid length and breadth, some good effigies, and a turret at the east end which is said to have been a watch-tower. One of the finest late-Gothic churches in the North, it has had good restoration work by many hands: Shepherd (1781), Dobson (1825), Salvin (1863), Hicks (1890s). St Paul's in Percy Street, is another large church (Salvin 1846); and the Presbyterian church in Lisburn Street (1840) is a nice element in the

The Green and Castle, BAMBURGH. (Two views)

Eighteenth-century lime kilns, BEADNELL

plain classical quarter in which it stands.

The Hotspur Gate (1450), a grim gateway in the now-vanished town walls, almost blocks the entrance to the inner town from the south-east (and is threatened with demolition). Pottergate Tower (1768 Gothick) is a nice example of a town folly (it originally had an open spire on top, like that of Newcastle Cathedral). The Town Hall (1771), in the attractively-sited small market-square, has an unusual and elegant tower. Lining one side of the square is the Assembly Rooms (Northumberland Hall), a handsome if austere building with shops in its arcaded ground floor, built in 1826 by an unrecorded architect: and in the square itself St Michael's Pant (or water supply), a stone column of 1765, has figures of St Michael and a dragon surmounting it. There is another fountain of St Michael and the dragon (1770) in Cannongate. Behind a fenced open-

ing in the wall of Rotten Row, a little out of the town centre, running from the parish church up to the castle estate-office, is a stone marking the place where William the Lion, of Scotland, was taken prisoner in 1174, while besieging the castle.

The Castle is enormous—and in its present form mostly late. It began as a motte-and-bailey, got a shell-keep later, came to the Percys in 1309; by the middle of the eighteenth century was ruinous: was made habitable in elegant Gothick by the first Duke with the help of Paine, Robert Adam and Shepherd; and was largely rebuilt for the fourth Duke by Salvin from 1854 onwards. The Gatehouse and Barbican are among the oldest parts (1310–20), with the figures of soldiers on the battlements (which cannot have deceived many attackers—the present figures being indeed eighteenth century). If baronial gothic outside, the castle is mostly Italian Renaissance

within. It is best seen from the Lion Bridge on the Berwick road (John Adam: 1773): and from the demesne running eastward from that, where it rises immense beyond the quiet waters of the Aln. The other bridges over the river are the Denwick Bridge (also by John Adam *c.* 1773) and the Canongate Bridge on the Eglingham road, 1821.

Just outside the town, to the north-west, the fourteenth-century gatehouse of *Alnwick Abbey* stands in a parkland setting: and 3½ miles farther on, at the end of an enchanting walk through a deep wooded glen, are the extensive remains of *Hulne Priory*, founded about 1240 and probably the first Carmelite monastery in England (with some eighteenth-century Gothic insertions) beside which is a Gothick summer-house of 1776. Both of these, and various other places and buildings of interest (such as the high eighteenth-century Gothic landscape feature of

Brizlee Tower; the eye-catcher gazebo by Robert Adam at Ratcheugh Cliffs; the Malcolm Cross, commemorating the death of the Scottish king at a siege of Alnwick in 1093), are situated in the vast castle demesnes which stretch for miles along the north of the town and are full of lovely tree-embowered walks. Alnwick, indeed, is surrounded by a wonderfully rich variety of scenery: immense splendidly-wooded parklands, soft pastoral country, grassy hills, heather-covered moorlands, wooded glens—and the sea four miles away.

Alwinton (7). The last lonely hamlet in Coquet-dale, beyond which the road winds through a narrowing glen. The church, on steeply sloping ground, has its twelfth–thirteenth century chancel 5 feet higher than its mid-nineteenth-century nave.

Clennell Hall, 1 mile north, is part fourteenth-century tower-house, partly late sixteenth-century, and mostly modern Tudor. There was once a hamlet here, as there was at Biddleston nearby, but they have long disappeared and the sites have been incorporated in private parklands.

There are a good many ancient remains about the neighbourhood. A mound of prehistoric stones, Russell's Cairn, right on the Border up on Windy Gyle (2034) named after a knight murdered by the Scots in 1585: forts at Gallow Law and Clennell Hill, an earthwork at Wholehope, hut circles at Dryhope Hill, cultivation terraces at Lord's Seat and Sharperton; and others. Clennell Street is one of the old drover roads from Scotland. Another goes by Bloodybush Edge (2,001 feet).

Amble (9). An old-established port at the mouth of the Coquet. Rows of mainly stone houses, all rather grim. *Thousands* of caravans.

Ancroft (2). A rather dim scattered Scottish-looking hamlet which was once a small town that made clogs and boots for Marlborough's armies. The barish Norman-founded but mainly nineteenth-century-restored church has a fourteenth-century peel for its tower.

Ashington (20). A large mostly twentieth-century mining town with rows of houses about a mile long, containing thousands of buildings and no architecture whatever. Famous for footballers.

Bamburgh (6). Dates from the dawn of English civilization. The capital seat of the Kings of Northumbria onwards from Ida, who, in 547 "built Bebhamburh which was at first inclosed by a hedge, and afterwards by a wall." Supposed to be the Joyous Gard whither Lancelot carried off Guinevere. Heavy with recorded ecclesiastical and secular history (sacked by the Danes in 993, besieged in 1095, again in the Wars of the Roses, etc.), it is now a pleasant village sloping down, from a grove of trees on a triangular green, towards the great basalt crags on which the castle is set.

The castle is enormous, a quarter of a mile long and covering 8½ acres of ground: perhaps the most tremendous spectacle of its kind in Britain. Though there has been a castle here since before the Conquest, the now visible parts, at least, are mostly eighteenth and nineteenth century: but that does not lessen their spectacular character. The castle dominates everything, village, countryside, sea, for miles around, with a terrific personality.

There has been a church here, at the top of the village, by the green, since 651; but the present building is chiefly thirteenth-century—and very fine and large it is, with a beautiful interior and a remarkable crypt. The unusually long chancel is said to be on the site of the Saxon church where St Aidan died in 651. Grace Darling is buried here: and there is a little memorial museum to her across the road.

There is some regrettable villadom to the north of the village and along the coast: but there are excellent sands, good fishing, a golf course: and Bamburgh is a good centre for trips to Holy Island, the Farne Islands, and the hills.

BELSAY

Bardon Mill (14). Though not much of a village, there is plenty of interest round about.

Housesteads and the best parts of the Roman Wall are 2 miles up the road; and on the way are *Chesterholme* (Vindolanda) where there was a Roman fort before the Wall was built, though the existing remains date mainly from the fourth century (and are of particular interest as showing changes from purely military use to soldier-farmer domesticity); and also *Barcombe* where there are British fortifications. Just before Vindolanda there is a Roman milestone opposite a farm on the banks of a small burn.

Willimoteswick, 1½ miles to the south-west, has a substantial tower of a fourteenth-century castle incorporated in a later house.

Allen Banks (1 mile to the east, where the river Allen joins the Tyne) is a 185-acre area of hill and valley scenery, with walks among wooded banks and crags, owned by the National Trust.

Beadnell (6). A scatter of bungalows, villas, holiday huts and shacks: but splendid sands. The church built about 1740, enlarged 1792, was redone in gothic in 1860. The group of eighteenth-century lime kilns by the rocky little harbour is owned by the National Trust.

Bedlington (14). The capital of Bedlingtonshire, a detached part of the Palatinate of Durham, until it was incorporated in Northumberland a century ago. Now a mining town, though the older part retains some grace and pleasantness in stone and pantiled houses facing a long wide Front Street with good trees and well-kept greens. There is an eighteenth-century obelisk; a sixteenth-century tower-house, a classical-fronted inn. The church, with a late Norman chancel arch, and some eighteenth-century work, is mostly nineteenth century and later. The ironworks here were pioneers in the making of rolled iron-rails; and made the rails for the first public railway—the Darlington and Stockton. There is a memorial inscription at the inn (the King's Arms) to Sir Daniel Gooch, the locomotive engineer, who also laid the Atlantic cables 1865–69. Two curiosities:

one, a stone in the church inscribed "Watson's Wake, 1669", a memorial to a man who climbed the church tower in his sleep and fell down and was killed when someone shouted and woke him: another, an epitaph on a stone in the churchyard:

Poems and epitaphs are but stuff
Here lies Robert Barras, that's
enough.

Bedlington terriers started here.

Belford (5). A trim little town on the Great North Road, the northern vista up the main street closed on the long frontage of an inn and the church. The church, with a Norman chancel arch, was much restored by Dobson and others. Belford Hall is by James Paine, 1756.

From the moorland road to Wooler there are grand views—eastward, the coast and the sea: westward, the Cheviots.

Bellingham (14) (pronounced, as in nearly all similar endings in the county, with a soft "g"). A small market town surrounded by rolling hills. Not much to look at: but it is an important little place, the "capital" of North Tyne country and Redesdale, and a good centre for seeing them. There are some old houses by the river: the church, with an early thirteenth-century chancel and chancel arch, was much rebuilt, but still in medieval form, about 1609: the bridge is by John Green, 1834. There are Romano-British inclosures in the neighbourhood. Hareshaw Linn is a 30-foot waterfall approached by a rough path up the winding Hareshaw Burn.

Hesleyside (1½ miles north-west) is a stately eighteenth-century house in parkland designed by Capability Brown, well seen from the road.

Up the long dale of the North Tyne there are ruined castles and peels on isolated sites: Tarset, Hole, Dalley, Gatehouse, Black Middings and others.

Belsay (23). The "village" is an example of what sometimes happened when a large land-owner set about improving his house and park. He bodily removed a village too near the manorial windows and rebuilt it at his park gates. That happened here in the 1830s–40s. The village is, in fact, only a charming row of

stone-built arcaded buildings along the roadside, most of them shops serving widely-scattered farmhouses.

Belsay Castle is one of the best examples in the county of a fourteenth-century single-tower castle, with a later house added in 1614; and is situated in a fine park near the early-nineteenth-century Greek mansion on the building of which John Dobson got his early training, assisting Sir Charles Monck.

West Bitchfield (isolated 1 mile south) is partly fifteenth-century tower and partly early seventeenth-century manor-house.

Beltingham (17). A hamlet grouped round a little green, with a Georgian house nearby and a small church (Tudor, over-restored in 1884), in a charming setting between the South Tyne and the river Allen, a mile south of Bardon Mill.

Berwick (2). Formerly in neither England nor Scotland, but a free town with its liberties extending a few miles up the coast and along the Tweed. As was inevitable for a key town pressed between contending nations, Berwick had a stormy history full of vicissitudes until the two countries at last united. Between 1147 and 1482 (when it was finally attached to the English crown) it changed hands thirteen times. Even then it was an important port and market town, as well as a strategic point. Its prosperity as a port continued until the development of the railway destroyed it, and now the broad estuary carries little more than a few fishing smacks; and the huge granaries and warehouses, huddled on narrow lanes, stand derelict and decayed. But its importance as the market town for a wide area of rich agricultural country on both sides of the Border continues; and today it is a lively and busy place.

It is also a place of great character, much interest and intricate changes of level. Seen from the other side of the Tweed, or from the train as it curves on to the high railway bridge from the south, it makes a picture

BERWICK:
The 16th-century walls
The Royal Border Bridge
(Robert Stephenson)
The three bridges

like a seventeenth-century engraving of some snug, trim Dutch port: in front the wide estuary crossed by noble bridges; and, beyond, a single spire-crowned tower riding above a brave display of pantiled roofs, rounded trees and city walls along the water's edge.

The defences are the most remarkable individual feature of the town. They are not merely of local but of European importance. With those of three other cities (Lucca, Verona and Antwerp) they were the first to be built to the post-medieval system of defence through curtain-walls and flanking bastions (which a century and more later was associated particularly with the name of Vauban). On a shorter circuit than the walls of Edward I, which for the most part they displaced (though they incorporated the earlier walls on the riverside section still to be seen on the cliff-side beyond Meg's Mount), they were begun about 1555 under Mary Tudor but mostly built from 1560 onwards at the command of Elizabeth, to the design of two Italian engineers, Portinari and Contio; and though they are the fourth in time to be built, they are in better preservation than the three earlier examples (indeed they are almost perfectly preserved). They are nearly a mile and a half long, and are 22 feet high, faced with precise and ponderous masonry, spectacularly strong. They were so strong that they were never needed to be used for their intended purpose: but in the four centuries since they were built they have served as a pleasant grass-verged promenade looking out, on the eastern half, over the open sea.

Just inside the fortifications, by Cow Port Gate on the eastern side, there are two other buildings of near-unique attraction. One is the parish church of the Holy Trinity, the only new church erected in England during the Commonwealth. Built by a London mason, John Young, its design was approved and its construction supervised (1648–52) by Colonel George Fenwick, a personal friend of Cromwell. It is one of the earliest

examples of a classical style in church building; and, though the exterior is not especially impressive (it has no tower), the interior has a fine dignity and restrained elegance. The chancel was added in 1855, and the reredos is the earliest known work of Sir Edwin Lutyens. The other of these two near-unique buildings is the Barracks, the earliest built in Britain. A striking quadrangle of buildings round a parade-ground, it was designed by, or under the supervision of, Vanbrugh and built between 1717 and 1721.

The Town Hall is the most prominent building, and externally the best: and it is strikingly placed, closing the lower end of the wide, gently-sloping Marygate, which divides round it to slope down towards the harbour by way of Hide Hill. It was built in 1757 and has generally been ascribed to Joseph Dods because he labelled himself "architect" on a stone over the entrance. But Dods was merely the building contractor: the real architects were Samuel and John Worrall of London.

Then there are the bridges, three of them, each noble of its kind. The Old Bridge (the sole southern entrance to the town until 1928, when the new bridge was opened) was built in 1611–24 of a beautifully coloured dark sandstone: a long, narrow, low-level bridge which *steps* sturdily nearly 1,200 feet across the broad estuary by fifteen ponderous arches 45 feet high. The high Royal Border Bridge, a railway bridge of almost Roman grandeur (by Robert Stephenson, 1847), proudly and long-leggedly *strides* across in fourteen 125-feet high arches (plus fourteen more on land). And the reinforced concrete New Bridge vaults somewhat heavily over 1,400 feet in four great flying *leaps*. The three of them together make a kind of Berwick Bridge symphony.

For the most part the town is built in a weather-darkened ashlar: but there are occasional light-painted façades, as in the lively range of buildings (the King's Arms, etc.) in Hide Hill, beyond the Town Hall from Marygate. There are many groups of good though rather severe and generally late "Georgian" houses (many of them actually dating from towards the middle of the nineteenth

century). The most closely integrated groups are in Ravensdowne and Quay Walls: but Bridge End, Bridge Street, Church Street, Marygate, Palace Green, Palace Street, Parade, West Street and Wool Market, among others, have many good northernly-plain buildings. The Art Gallery has pictures by Raeburn, Allan Ramsay, Degas and others.

If the twentieth century has made a brave even if somewhat heavy-handed contribution in the New Bridge, it has committed an unspeakable horror at the end of it, in a bus-station that makes a beastly blood-red hole in the town at its most vital place. Whoever "designed" it should be run over by every bus that calls there.

North-west of the town, almost on the Border, is Hallidon Hill, where the Scots won a bloody battle in 1333; and where now there is a great view with Berwick near at hand, the coast stretching out 20 miles from Eyemouth to the Farnes, Cheviot 20 miles to the south, the Eildons 30 miles westward and the Lammermuirs completing the circle.

Birtley (14). A rebuilt estate-hamlet high up beyond the river from Wark-on-Tyne. The small church (restored 1884) has a Norman chancel arch. In the garden of the vicarage is a ruined "Vicar's Peel" of 1611. Northwards a Holy Well and waterfall, and the Devil's Stone with the Devil's hoofmarks where he tried to jump the river and landed into Leap Crag Pool. On the hill above that is Male Knock Camp, a conspicuous earthwork with traces of hut circles.

There are earthworks of no less than seven camps in the neighbourhood, including Good Wife Hot Camp, Night Folds, Shieldene, Carryhouse, Barrows on the Pitland Hills and Low Shield Green.

Blanchland (25). One of the most perfect examples in England of a "planned" village. Not that there is any documentary evidence to show that it was planned, but the material evidence is undeniable: its level eaves and ridge lines and similar frontages prove that it must have been built more or less as a single undertaking.

It is said that it is built on the foundations of the buildings of the disestablished monastic house, but that is unlikely. It was built in its present form by some unknown genius in the late eighteenth or early nineteenth century, probably to house workers in the then prosperous lead mines in the hills round about.

The village consists of cottages of warm-coloured stone with stone-slab roofs built round a gravel-surfaced double square, in shape like a heavily-thickened L. The pant, or covered pump, is situated in a position to compose the two parts. But though it has this remarkable quality, there is nothing precious about the place: and fortunately it is almost unspoiled.

The church is what remains of the abbey which, after its dissolution in 1539 stood neglected and ruinous for nearly 200 years until it was bought and repaired by Lord Crewe, Bishop of Durham. The interior is of fine many-coloured stone work, with a high noble arch to the tower. Like the village, the nave also is L-shaped. The monastic gateway is still one of the entrances to the village square. The inn is in part the thirteenth-century guest-house of the abbey. It was the home of the Forster family until it was forfeited by General Forster for his part in the Jacobite Rising of 1715.

The setting is perfect for such a place. Entirely secluded and set among fine trees in the deep glen of the upper Derwent, the village is approached in every direction over wild moorland. But being so unusual and so romantically situated, it has too many visitors at weekends; and nowadays it is better to see it on a weekday during the less popular months of the year.

A story says that in 1327, on one of their many raids, the Scots missed it because of its secluded situation: and the monks rang a peal of bells in thanksgiving for deliverance—but prematurely; for the Scots heard the bells and came back and sacked the place.

Some miles downstream the river has been dammed for a large lake-

Above:
BLANCHLAND

Below:
Farm near BOLAM. The round threshing barn is a local type

CHIPCHASE *Castle*

reservoir; and a great new feature has thus been added to the landscape.

Blyth (24). A busy port exporting coal (though to a decreasing extent), importing timber; and a mining town. A workaday place with two good modern parish churches, a Presbyterian church with a good brick spire, and a few eighteenth-century houses near the harbour and in the main street of its suburb, Cowpen. Near the harbour there are some pleasant gardens: and there is a pretty lighthouse of 1788. The first of all English "railways" was laid down here in the early seventeenth century to take the coal from the nearby Bebside pit to the river, horses drawing coal-waggons along parallel beams of wood.

Bolam (22). Once a town with a castle and "two hundred slated houses enclosing a green". The town and castle have utterly vanished, and only the church and its vicarage remain, with a fine Saxon tower and Norman nave, standing in a church-yard which gives a lovely view towards Angerton, Wallington and the Simonside Hills. In the south aisle of the church is a tiny window

showing the spot where a bomb jettisoned by a German plane on May 1st, 1942 entered the building but fortunately did not explode.

Bolam House is on the site of the demolished castle, which was itself built inside a British camp. Bolam Lake, in the park, is said to be designed by Dobson. Shortflatt, a mile to the south, is a thirteenth-century peel with a later house attached. There are fine trees on the approach road to the village from the south, and all about.

There are several camp sites near by: and there is a 6-feet high standing stone (Poind and His Man: but the second stone has been removed and stands in a field towards Wallington) beside a barrow on the moorland to the west.

Bothal (23). A small tree-embowered hamlet in the glen of the Wansbeck, with a fine small castle of the tower-house type (fourteenth century) in a commanding position; and a little church (early thirteenth century) which has a curious triple bell-tower and, inside, the columns all awry, the nave oddly shaped, fragments of fourteenth-century glass, some fine altar rails and a magnificent sixteenth-

BRINKBURN PRIORY

century alabaster table-tomb. It all makes a lovely oasis in this sad and sour part of the county.

There is a splendid railway viaduct in the woods a mile to the west.

Boulmer (9). The old hamlet, once a notorious smuggling place, was a few fishermen's houses, a farmhouse or two, and blue-painted boats on the green facing the sea; but the Air Force Warning Station and its houses have made a different kind of place.

Branxton (4). A small village among hillocky cornfield country under Cheviot. Here on a September evening in 1513 was fought the fearful battle of Flodden, when a hastily-levied army of 26,000 northern English (the main army being with the King in France at the time) defeated a much larger Scottish army with dreadful slaughter (at least 15,000 men being killed). The place is marked by a modern monument bearing the simple inscription TO THE BRAVE OF BOTH NATIONS.

The church, with Norman chancel arch and a stumpy stone spire is mostly neo-Norman of 1849. Pallinsburn is a modern mansion at the end of a long avenue through a wooded park. At Howtell, a hamlet 2 miles south, is the ruin of a fifteenth-century tower.

The King's Stone, in a field by the road to Cornhill, is a prehistoric monolith, 7 feet high.

Brinkburn Priory (20). Exquisitely situated among trees in a park in the dene of a secluded loop of the Coquet below Rothbury, this beautiful twelfth-century church of an almost cathedral dignity was a roofless ruin in 1858. It was then wonderfully-well restored by Thomas Austin, a young Durham architect, and is probably the best Gothic church in Northumberland. It is now in the guardianship of the Ministry of Public Building and Works and can again be visited. The handsome partly late-Georgian and partly romantic early nineteenth-century house adjoining is falling to ruin.

Byrness (11). The first part of a new village for the Forestry Commission, built in terraces facing a series of irregularly-shaped greens: but left less than half-finished. There is a modest little chapel-of-ease (1786) down the road. The rapidly growing forest spreads all about the surrounding hills.

This is the last village before Scotland. The road goes on past Catcleugh Reservoir (supplying Newcastle) to the crossing of the Border at Carter Bar: and the *Pennine Way* starts

here on its longest stretch, a hard, lonely 27-mile walk, by Ravens-knowe (1,729 feet), Chew Green, Windy Gyle (2,034 feet) and Auchope Cairn, to Kirk Yetholm on the Scottish side.

Chew Green (marked as Ad Fines on most maps, and called Golding Pots in medieval times) is the finest visible group of Roman earthworks in Britain. Away in the hills on the very Border, and miles from any-where, its wild situation adds to its intrinsic interest. As well as by walking the Pennine Way, it can be approached, to within shorter walking distance, by car over military roads (with permission) from Birdhope, near High Rochester, via Silloans and Featherwood, as far as Foulplay Head.

Bywell (27). One of the most interesting spots in Northumberland.

A passage from the report of the Royal Commissioners in 1570 gives a vivid picture not only of what it was then, but also of the condition of the county as far south as this even at that late date. "The town of Bywell is builded in length all of one street upon the river or water of Tyne, on the north and west part of the same; and it is divided into several parishes, and inhabited with handicraftsmen, whose trade is all in iron work for the horsemen and Borderers of that country, as in making of bits, stirrups, buckles and such others, wherein they are very expert and cunning: and are subject to the incursions of the thieves of Tynedale, and compelled winter and summer to bring all their cattle and sheep into the street at night time, and watch both ends of the street: and when the enemy approacheth to raise hue and cry, whereupon all the town prepareth for rescue of their goods; and which is very populous by reason of their trade, and stout and hardy by continual practice against the enemy.''

Every sign of the town has gone, and Bywell now consists of *two* ancient parish churches, a castle, a mansion, a farm, a vicarage, a medieval market cross, and not another building in sight—all situated at the secluded head of a cul-de-sac in a wooded bend of the Tyne and surrounded by fine parkland.

St Andrew's (the westerly church, called the White Church because it belonged to the White Canons of Blanchland) has one of the best Saxon towers in the county, though the rest, with transepts and very short nave, is a good deal rebuilt: St Peter's (the Black Church because it belonged to the Black Monks of Durham) is part eleventh century, but chiefly thirteenth, with three fine lancet east windows. The castle, built of Roman stones, is a substantial building of the tower-house type, dating from the fifteenth century. The Hall, standing back from the road, within a park, designed by James Paine in 1760, was altered and added to by Dobson in 1817. The vicarage dates from 1698.

Cambo (15). A well-kept small enclosed estate village, planned and begun in 1740, well situated, just off the main road, with contrasting views of the wooded valley of Wansbeck on one side, and wilder open country on the other. The post-office is in a medieval tower-house. The modest church (1842) has a tall tower (1883) and standing on high ground is a feature of the surrounding landscape.

Wallington (1 mile south). A late seventeenth-century mansion built

St Andrew's, BYWELL

by Sir William Blackett; in a fine park with magnificent trees; now, through the generosity of the Trevelyan family, held by the National Trust, together with 13,000 acres and most of the village of Cambo. The house has good rococo plasterwork, fine porcelain, furniture and pictures. The courtyard was roofed over, in 1855, by Dobson (on the advice of Ruskin) and decorated with paintings by Bell Scott, with one decoration by Ruskin himself. The stable block is very elegant, with a pedimented centre surmounted by a large lantern with a cupola on an open rotunda of columns. The gardens, which are half a mile away from the house, were laid out by Capability Brown (who began his work here as an apprentice) in 1766. The house and park are well seen over a ha-ha from the road to the east (the bridge is by James Paine, 1760); and are open at weekends during the summer.

The Blackett family not only developed the house and grounds: they also created wide improvements over their great estate, enclosing land, building farmhouses, making roads.

At Rothley, nearly 3 miles north of the house, two towers (Rothley Castle) were built in 1776 solely as scenic eye-catchers, while Cadger's Fort had a more serious intent, as a defence against the Stuart menace in 1745 though it was never tested as such. There was a great deer park in the wild country about Rothley Crags.

Capheaton (22). A row of eighteenth-century cottages at the gates to Capheaton Hall: a fine tree-lined approach from the north; a southward

Wallington, CAMBO: the courtyard

prospect over a lake. Off the beaten track.

The Hall (1668, by Robert Trollope) is an interesting and architecturally important building, at once plain Northern but with fanciful carved detail to doorways, window-surrounds etc. The grounds, certainly the lake, were probably landscaped by Capability Brown.

The Swinburne family lived here from the thirteenth century onwards. The poet, though born in the south, was much attached to Northumberland and often stayed in his grandfather's house here.

Carham (4). A roadside estate-hamlet with trim hedges, on the Tweed in a corner tipping into Scotland. Late eighteenth-century church. Forts at Downham and Moneylaws Castle Hill.

There was a battle here in 833, between the English and the Danes, at which, according to Leland "eleven bishops and two English counts were slain and a great number of people". And it was here in 1018 that Malcolm II of Scotland won the battle which decided that it was the Tweed, not the Forth, as hitherto, that was to be the boundary between England and Scotland.

Catton (17). A well-kept substantial village on the hillside, looking over East Allendale: but a ribbon of houses towards Allendale Town compromising it.

Chatton (5). A long neat street of mostly one-storey cottages, with a green at the foot, and view of the moors down the road. An eighteenth-century church, thoroughly Victorianized.

Fowberry Tower, 1 mile north-west, is an eighteenth-century house built around a seventeenth-century house which incorporated a sixteenth-century tower-house.

There are ten contour camps and three earthworks in the neighbourhood: and Chatton Law has cup-and-ring carvings on its summit.

Chillingham (5) (pron. hard g). A hamlet insignificant in itself, but with a church and castle of great interest. The church was a small bare twelfth-century building, singularly stark, until it was restored in 1966

by John Smith. A rickety little gallery and panelling had to go in the restoration, which was a pity: but the restoration and alterations have been well done: the south transept which had been interrupted by a screen to the Gray memorial tomb has been given its proper spacial effect, and a perfectly devised clear-glazed east window has been inserted beyond a modern altar and modern furnishings. The transepts and chancel are five steps above the nave, because of a crypt below. The bell-cote is of 1753.

Wallington, CAMBO: the stables

The great feature of the church is the magnificent richly-carved fifteenth-century table tomb of Sir Ralph Gray and his wife—one of the finest of its kind in the country. Dating from about 1450, it has fourteen figures of saints in niches separated by figures of angels, a rich canopy, alabaster figures and a reredos.

The castle, dating from 1344, consisted originally of four angle towers connected by curtain walls, but various additions and alterations since (the last extensive ones by

Wyatville: 1828) made it a complicated as well as interesting building. It is now falling into decay.

The vast park, of great beauty, very old, and embracing every kind of scenery from woodland to high moorland, still has in it a few head of the famous herd of wild cattle, part of which has now gone to Whipsnade. "The cattle are believed to be directly descended from the Wild Ox, *Bos taurus*, which roamed the country in prehistoric times. Written records of the herd go back for a very long period; and there is no history of the introduction of any domesticated blood. The animals are left entirely to their own devices, except that they are supplied with hay in the winter. They retain many wild characteristics. They are prone to stampede when approached by human beings, and if an animal is caught and handled by man and then turned loose again, it will be expelled by the herd and may be gored to death. The herd is ruled by the most powerful bull, the 'King Bull', and he is the father of all the calves born during his reign. When his powers begin to decline he is challenged to fight by one of the younger bulls. Sometimes a single fight decides the issue, but occasionally a series of fights takes place. If the contest does not result in the death of the old King Bull he is driven out of the herd, and, living a solitary existence, he soon pines away and dies." (From a note by T. Russell Goddard.)

Hepburn Tower, 1 mile south-east, is a well-preserved bastle-house of the fifteenth century.

Ros Castle, 1½ miles east, up the very steep hillside from Hepburn on the grand moorland road towards North Charlton and the coast, is a hilltop owned by the National Trust. There are tremendous views: Chillingham Park, Till Valley and Cheviots on one side: Holy Island, Farne Island, Bamburgh and a great arc of the sea on the other. There is also an elegant transmission pylon near the summit at Botany.

Chipchase (14). Estate-hamlet and castle, 1½ miles south-east of Wark-on-Tyne. The castle, one of the finest

CAPHEATON Hall. A detail, 1668

The CHILLINGHAM Cattle

mansions in the county, is a splendid combination of a large-scale mid-fourteenth-century tower with a distinguished Jacobean house of 1621, and Georgian additions and alterations. In the park is a mid-eighteenth-century chapel with box pews and a double-decker pulpit. The village church is early nineteenth century.

Chollerford (15). A well-known inn and a fine bridge (of 1771) in a well-wooded part of the North Tyne valley.

Chesters. The extensive and extensively excavated remains of Cilurnum are perhaps the most interesting and certainly most beautifully situated of all the forts on the Wall. The fort housed a cavalry regiment 500 strong.

Foundations of sections of the enclosing wall, barracks, headquarters, Commandant's house, bath-house and the abutments of the bridge have been excavated. The museum at the park gates contains a notable collection of Roman stones and objects.

The mansion is a house of 1771 much enlarged by Norman Shaw in 1891.

CHILLINGHAM: fifteenth-century tomb of Sir Ralph Gray

Chollerton (15). A quiet hamlet with an externally unimpressive church which has five Roman monolithic columns in its south twelfth-century arcade; a font which is a re-used Roman altar, and a seventeenth-century organ. There are many camps, earthworks and hut circles in the neighbourhood.

Cocklaw Tower (1 mile south-east) is the well-preserved ruin of a fifteenth-century peel-tower.

Coanwood (16). A colliery village of the small isolated and now abandoned Haltwhistle coalfield.

At *Burn House*, 3 miles eastward, there is a lonely Friends Meeting House of 1760 standing in a little graveyard on the hillside close to a farm.

Coquet Island (21). A mile off the mouth of the River Coquet and the port of Amble, its 80-feet high lighthouse (built in 1841) being a prominent feature for miles either way along the coast. The island has had long religious associations. Bede records it as a meeting place for monks. Here, in 684, Cuthbert accepted his bishopric. The remains of a chapel and priests' cell are incorporated into the light-house-keeper's cottage. All signs of the tower-house recorded in 1415 have disappeared. The island is a breeding place for eider ducks, locally called St Cuthbert's ducks.

Corbridge (18–22). A pleasant small town with a long and sometimes stormy history—Ethelred, King of Northumbria, was slain here in A.D. 796; King Ragnal, the Dane, defeated the English and Scots in 918; and the town was occupied by David I of Scotland in 1138, and was burned by William Wallace in 1296, by Robert Bruce in 1312, and by David II in 1346. It is well situated on the rising north bank of the Tyne at the head of a sloping seven-arched bridge of 1674. On the east

Roman arch re-used in CORBRIDGE church. Relief in the museum at Corstopitum

Roman Corstopitum. CORBRIDGE in the distance

side of the bridge, the road to Newcastle is wide and fronted by good stone houses; and its end narrows so that the view out is closed where a house of 1700 leans against a tower-house of, probably, the sixteenth century. About the middle, facing the bridge, is the long-fronted Angel Inn, one of the oldest in the county, the present building having a seventeenth-century central part and Georgian and later additions and alterations. On the west side of the bridge-head, beyond a sharp turn along a narrow street where the shops are, the Market Place is fronted by the most important Saxon building in Northumberland, standing back a little among trees in its churchyard. The lower part of the unusually slender tower dates from some time before 786, and the upper part probably from about 970, after the church had been ravaged by the Danes; the nave has walls with a seventh-century core, with some Norman work and the rest thirteenth century: at the east end, and also in the north transept, are three slim lancet windows. But the most remarkable feature is the interior tower arch, taken from the Roman gateway at Corstopitum and rebuilt here in its entirety. The fortified vicarage in the churchyard, dating from about 1300, is also built of Roman stones from Corstopitum. Also in the Market Place is an interesting cast-iron market cross of 1814, and a stone well-head.

Corstopitum (1½ miles north-west) is the site of an important Roman stores base and supply town, which was several times over-run, sacked and rebuilt in times of warfare. Extensive foundations have been laid open; and remains are exhibited in a museum attached to the site. The relics of the Roman bridge are still visible when the river is low.

Dilston Castle (1½ miles south-west) is the substantial remains of the castle always associated with one of the most romantic of Northumbrian figures, the young Earl of Derwentwater, executed for his part in the 1715 rising.

Aydon Castle (2 miles north-east) is a fine late-thirteenth- or early-fourteenth-century fortified manor-

Dunstanburgh Castle, CRASTER, from the north

house, splendidly situated above a deep ravine and of outstanding historical and architectural importance for its design of domestic comfort at so early a date. Nearby is a house of the late seventeenth century.

Halton Tower (3 miles north) is a fourteenth-century smaller tower-house, built of Roman stones, with fifteenth- and seventeenth-century wings attached to it; and, a little distance away, a small bare Jacobean chapel with an early Norman chancel arch.

Beaufront Castle (2 miles north-west) is a magnate's castle of 1840, by Dobson, standing in fine parkland, and a prominent feature of the landscape in this part of the Tyne valley.

Cornhill (4). The last, rather commonplace village in England on the middle (Wooler) road. A mile beyond, the road crosses the Tweed into Scotland, by a fine five-arched bridge built by Smeaton in 1763.

Cramlington (23). A mining town now in course of being revivified by the addition of new town development. The older parts are mostly typical featureless long rows of miners' houses; the new ones look strange and gimmicky beside them: each type seems to bring out the more extreme features of the other. But perhaps they will settle down together. Meanwhile it is an unusual example of new town creation because it is being undertaken by the County Council and not, as is more usual, on central government initiative.

Craster (9). A fishing hamlet in a craggy landscape. Bright painted boats and lobster pots in an exciting little harbour. Famous for kippers.

Craster Tower is a tower-house with Georgian additions.

Dunstan, immediately nearby, is one of the three places claiming to be the birthplace of Duns Scotus (*c.* 1265).

Dunstanburgh (1½ miles north, by a field path along the coast). The impressive ruins of a great early-fourteenth-century fortress, spectacularly situated on the edge of the dark dolerite crags above a now blocked-up harbour which once

sheltered the royal navy of Henry VIII.

Cullernose Point (1 mile south) is the 120-foot high headland where the Whin Sill meets the sea.

Cresswell (21). A hamlet by a rocky reef with firm sands and sand-dunes stretching northwards in the great sweep of Druridge Bay. A fourteenth-century peel-tower on the edge of the park of a vanished mansion of which only the stables, with a clock tower (1821) remain. The church is neo-Norman of 1836.

Crookham (4). A hamlet on the river Till. Immediately by Flodden, it is memorable besides because here, as late as 1678, occurred the last border affray between the English and the Scots.

Cullercoats (24). Joined up now with Whitley Bay and Tynemouth, and physically almost indistinguishable from them except for a few old cottages remaining, the old fishing village still retains something of an aura of its former detached self. It is still a fishing place: and it has a delightful little harbour. The fish-wives of Cullercoats, with their distinctive and picturesque costume had a special place in Northumberland coast lore but have disappeared within the last decade or two. The church (Pearson, 1884) gives a fine point of accent to the sea-front; and is said to be the only church in the North (excluding Durham Cathedral) to be vaulted in stone throughout.

Denwick (9). An estate hamlet of about 1850 and a good bridge over the Aln, towards Alnwick.

Doddington (5). A scattered village at the foot of Dod Law, and looking over to Cheviot. The ruined but substantial tower-house was one of the last to be built (1584) before the Union with Scotland. The thirteenth-century but completely re-arranged church, which is difficult to find, has a pretty interior of grey and pink stone. In the churchyard there is a stone watch-house built in 1826 against body snatchers.

On Dod Law there are British camps; and, particularly at Ringses Camp, examples of the mysterious rock tracings called "cup-and-ring

The stables of the vanished mansion at CRESSWELL

marking". There are also hill and valley camps in the neighbourhood: and at Rowting Lynn an important earthwork in a miniature gorge, and other cup-and-ring markings. On the south of the hill is a 20-foot high block of stone with vertical grooving on it, said by legend to have been made by the chain with which the Devil hanged his grandmother there. Near the stone is Cuddy's Cave, traditionally associated with St Cuthbert who is said to have lived in these parts as a boy.

Duddo (4). An insignificant hamlet with a fragment of a tower-house in a commanding position on a craggy knoll. Half a mile away is a group of five megalithic standing-stones, 5–10 feet high.

Earsdon (24). In the sad coalfield area, a village which still keeps some character and a few pleasant Georgian houses. A fine church of 1836 (John and Benjamin Green) in a dominating position and with a big tower. In the churchyard is an obelisk "erected to the memory of 204 miners who lost their lives in Hartley Pit . . . 16th January 1862". In a great common grave 159, some of them children of 11 and 12, are buried here. Hartley, a grim colliery village, is three miles away, near the coast.

Edlingham (9). A hillside hamlet in a small green valley surrounded by moors. The rude little church has a tower of semi-military character; a Norman porch and doorway; and

Terrace houses: Simpson Street, CULLERCOATS

a Norman chancel arch and north aisle. The ruin of a late-fourteenth-century tower-house beside the banks of the Edlingham Burn has a fire-place much illustrated in textbooks of English medieval architecture.

The five-arched viaduct of a dis-used railway makes a strong incident in the landscape around the hamlet: and there is an enormous panorama of Cheviot and adjoining hills from the climbing road to the north-east.

Eglingham (8). A small roadside village near the wooded banks of the Eglingham Burn, with some detached bits of moorland in the background. The church, on the site of an earlier building of 738, has a tower of about 1200, now with a pointed lead-covered roof, a chancel rebuilt in the early seventeenth century, a nave also rebuilt about 1660 after being burned by the Scots in the Civil War—all much restored in Victorian times, and now rather bare and severe.

The Hall, on the site of a peel tower, has parts from the sixteenth century but is mostly from 1704.

The Ringses is a circular contour earthwork, with three massive ram-parts and hut circles in the enclosure, on Beanley Moor, to the south. There are many other forts in the neighbourhood—Preacher's Knowe, Jenny's Lantern Hill, Beanley Hill, Titlington Mount, Shipley Moor.

Ellingham (6). A few houses and one or two larger ones nearby, looking over the flat coastal plain just off the Great North Road: a church of 1862: and, attached to the Hall, a Roman Catholic chapel of 1897, successor to one described by the Jesuit in charge, in 1750, when the penal laws were still in force, as having "about 150 customers to my shop".

Elsdon (12). A large triangular green, a few houses, mainly eighteenth-century, about the sides, and all around a landscape of rolling grassy hills. The curiously bell-turreted fourteenth-century church has a fine bare interior, with extraordinarily narrow aisles less than a yard wide, and some good wall-tablets: all seen in a liquid kind of light that comes through the clear-glazed tree-shaded windows. The clear-glazing of the east window is especially effective, with tree branches seen waving gently beyond the altar.

To the north of the church there is a fourteenth-century vicar's peel or fortified rectory. Also, to the east, a well-preserved and particularly fine example of a Norman hill-motte-and-bailey of about 1080.

Elsdon was the capital centre of Redesdale and all this part of the Border. When the church was being restored in 1810, rows of over 100 male skeletons were found buried along the north wall of the church, thought to be those of some of the

EDLINGHAM Church and Castle

men who fought in the Battle of Otterburn (1388). There is a bull-baiting stone on the green, and the remains of a cock-pit.

To the south-east, on the side road towards Rothley, 1,040 feet up, where there is one of the greatest views in Northumberland, are the remains of the Steng Cross, probably an early landmark to travellers, and also the remains of a gibbet of 1791: and off the road, to the north, Manside Camp, a strong earthwork, with double ditches and intervallum. Northwards on the hills towards the Border are numerous earthworks, camps, cairns and other ancient remains.

The road over to Hepple, towards Rothbury, has splendid hill views.

Embleton (6). An average village near the coast, with a good thirteenth-century church and a fourteenth-century fortified rectory.

Embleton Bay is a fine stretch of sands crowned at its southern end by Dunstanburgh castle and crags.

Etal (4). A charming estate village with stone and white-washed walls, and surprising thatch as well as slates and pantiles for roofing; and cottage gardens. At one end the entrance gates to the eighteenth-century Hall, with a chapel of 1858 by Butterfield in its splendid grounds; at the other end, facing them down the village, some substantial remains of a fourteenth-century castle guarded by two guns from Cowper's *Royal George*. All surrounded by trees on a small bank above the Till, with views of Cheviot and the Border from near about.

Falstone (11). Just off the little-used road to Scotland via Kielder, a hamlet with a few houses, two churches, a school, a shop or two and an inn, which served the scattered farms and cottages of the upper parts of North Tynedale before the coming of the Forestry Commission. Remote among the hills.

Farne Islands (6). A famous group of about thirty rocky islands, totalling some 80 acres in extent, between two and five miles off the coast opposite Bamburgh. Now the property of the National Trust.

The nearest island, the Inner Farne,

was in early times a retreat of religious mystics. St Aidan was here in 651; and St Cuthbert lived here between 676 and 685, and from 687 till his death in 688. Later, from about 1255 till the Dissolution, the monastery of Durham had a regular cell of two monks here. The existing small chapel of St Cuthbert is what remains of the church that is known to have been built about 1370. Near by is the ruin of a small tower-house built about 1500.

The farthest island of any extent is the Longstone, where Grace Darling with her father, keeper of the lighthouse which still stands there (built 1826), rowed out on her brave deed of rescue in September 1838.

"The Farne islands constitute the most interesting bird sanctuary in the British Isles. The Eider Duck, Cormorant, Shag, Lesser Black-backed Gull, Herring Gull, Kittiwake Gull, Sandwich Tern, Arctic Tern, Common Tern, Roseate Tern, Fulmar Petrel, Oyster-catcher, Ringed Plover, Razorbill, Common Guillemot and Puffin all breed here during the summer. Eider Ducks have bred on the Farne Islands from time immemorial; and ancient manuscripts inform us that these birds were known to St Cuthbert and were protected by him whilst he lived on the Inner Farne. The Terns, commonly called 'sea-swallows' owing to their long pointed wings and deeply-forked tails, are migrants. They spend the winter in the southern hemisphere, and come up to the islands, many thousands strong, every summer to rear their young. The Arctic Tern is perhaps the most remarkable of all birds from the point of view of migration. A nest of this species has been found only 450 miles from the North Pole in the summer, whereas the winter range of the species extends well into the Antarctic region. The flat tops of the Pinnacle Rocks are densely packed with Guillemots throughout the summer. . . . The most interesting carnivore is the Grey Seal. This is the largest and rarest of the British seals. Its only breeding place on the eastern side of Great Britain is at the Farne Islands. Mature bull Grey Seals may be 10 feet long and weigh 650 lb.; the cows are considerably smaller and lighter. The young are born in November or December, and at birth

they are covered with a coat of creamy-white woolly hair. This is shed when they are about six weeks old (at which time they take to the sea), disclosing a coat of shorter hair, which is in varying shades of grey, and spotted." (From a note by T. Russell Goddard.)

The islands may be reached by motor boat from Seahouses or Bamburgh. The best time to visit is the end of May or early June.

Felton (20). A large village on the Great North Road above the wooded banks of the Coquet, the old medieval bridge now being by-passed and preserved. There is a good thirteenth–fourteenth-century church where, during restoration in 1870, seventy skulls were found lying together with spurs and Scottish coins. It has a massive primitive-looking bell-cote, a rugged porch with a rib-and-slab roof, and in the five-light fourteenth-century window at the east end of the south aisle three elaborately-carved roundels cut from a single stone.

North of the village, at the side of a section of the now by-passed old Great North Road, is an obelisk of 1807 commemorating Nelson in "memory of private friendship".

Ford (4–5). The village has sometimes been called the "prettiest village in Northumberland"; but it is singularly unpleasant, being a bit of nineteenth-century suburban Surrey planted into these foreign parts. It is also aggressively model.

The corner-towered castle was first built in the early fourteenth century, rebuilt at the beginning of the seventeenth, Strawbery-hilled in the eighteenth (under the advice of Robert Adam) and re-medievalised in the nineteenth: but two of the original four towers remain. It is now a holiday home for boys.

The church, badly restored by Dobson in 1853, is of early thirteenth-century foundation and has a massive bell-cote of a rare type. Nearby is the ruin of a fortified vicarage. The churchyard and the lanes on this side of the village, give splendid views over Flodden Field towards the Cheviots. On the other side there are fine trees.

FARNE ISLANDS

Fourstones (15). A scattered quarrying village in pleasant country, to which a considerable colony of semis has been regrettably attached.

Gilsland (13). A hillocky hamlet right on the county boundary in bare open country, and right on the Roman Wall where it enters Cumberland; with mysterious monstrous shapes of things connected with war about the sky-line of the secret War Department expanse of Spadeadam Waste.

Glanton (8). A fairly large average village in good country on a bumpy ridge which divides the valleys of the Breamish and the Aln. It has no church within its boundaries; but has a bird research station. There are curious radar-equipment shapes on the hills to the south.

Crawley Tower (1½ miles northeast) has an early-fourteenth-century tower-house incorporated in a later house and stands at the corner of a rectangular earthwork.

Gosforth (23). A suburb-satellite to Newcastle, north of the great Town Moor, Gosforth claims to be a separate place, but it is impossible to tell where it begins and Newcastle ends. There are one or two urban terraces of the early nineteenth century, but it is mostly later "villa" streets. The parish church, St Nicholas, is late classical of 1799 by John Dodds, with aisles put in by Dobson in 1818, and the chancel rebuilt in 1913. All Saints is a good late-Victorian church by R. J. Johnson, 1887. Salters Bridge, across the Ouseburn, has a medieval arch.

Gosforth House, a large classical house designed by James Paine, *c.* 1760, was burned down by suffragettes in 1914, and restored in 1921. Newcastle races are run in the fine parkland surrounding the house, and the house is used as part of the grandstand.

Greenhead (13), on the Tipalt Burn, at the junction of the Newcastle–Carlisle road and the Military road, near the western boundary of the county, close by the Roman Wall where it goes up and down the Nine Nicks of Thirlwall (though the western part of that, above Greenhead, has in recent years been destroyed by quarrying for whinstone). In the centre of the village the church, by Dobson, 1826, has a spire; and by the bridge is a farmhouse, once a coaching inn, with a classical doorway and pediment dated 1757.

Thirlwall Castle (1 mile north) is a tall picturesque ruin of a mid-fourteenth-century tower-house, standing above the Tipatt. *Blenkinsop Castle* (1 mile south) was originally built in the fourteenth century but mostly rebuilt and extended in the nineteenth. Both of these buildings and many farmhouses and cottages hereabouts were built of stone plundered from the Wall.

Carvoran, the Roman fort Magna, has been largely destroyed by farming. There are various other camp sites nearby.

FORD Forge

HALTWHISTLE

Up on the Wall, at 950 feet, to-wards Walltown House, is a great all-round view—to the east the Wall itself running out towards Serving Shields, to the south the Tyne valley and the hills beyond, to the west Cumberland and a glimpse of the Solway, to the north the Northumberland hills and, beyond the county boundary, the wide expanse of Spadeadam Waste now dangerous for other reasons than its mere desolation.

Guyzance (9). A small trim estate hamlet on the banks of the Coquet. A ruined chapel in a walled graveyard close to the long stone bridge: and a mill of 1775 nearby.

Haltwhistle (16–17). A substantial roadside town, now by-passed, in fine South Tynedale country, once the market town of a small isolated and now worked-out coalfield which is singularly injured by its mining. It has an excellent thirteenth-century church almost hidden by houses. The Roman Wall and the fort at Great Chesters (Aesica) are 1½–2 miles to the north.

Bellister Castle (1 mile south) is the ruin of a sixteenth-century bastel-house with a house of 1669 attached.

Featherstone Castle (3 miles south-west), one of the most impressive in Northumberland, one of the most beautifully situated in its large wooded grounds by the South Tyne,

and with one of the bloodiest his-tories, has some part from the thir-teenth century, with a strong tower-house of 1330, but the major part built about 1810. The nearby bridge, in one steep arch, dates from 1775.

Park is a roadside hamlet on the approach to Featherstone.

Harbottle (7). The last village in Coquetdale; once the capital of the Middle March, and heavy with his-torical associations. A few stone houses, overtopped by a fragment of a mid-twelfth-century castle on a green knoll; a rocky river with pools; woods; pastoral vale; and hills all round.

On Harbottle Crag is the Drake

Stone, a 30-foot-high mass of sandstone associated with Druidal and other ancient rites; and beyond that the lonely water of Harbottle Lough.

Harlow Hill (22). The first hamlet of a few houses where the line of the Wall becomes the Military Road. On the west below the hill are century-old reservoir-lakes supplying the Newcastle district with water. Nearby these is Welton Hall, a ruined fifteenth-century peel tower built of Roman stones, with a manor house of 1614 attached.

Hartburn (19–22). An attractive small village above the steep wooded banks of the Hart Burn. The fine spacious two-aisled church of warm-coloured stone, is thirteenth century (the tower late twelfth), with various monuments including one by Chantry, and a tablet to John Hodgson, a distinguished historian of Northumberland, who was a vicar here from 1833 to 1845: also a good window (1942) in the south aisle by L. C. Evetts. There is a tower built as a school and schoolmaster's house by Dr Sharp, who was vicar from 1749 to 1796. The track of The Devil's Causeway, a mysterious Roman road running from the Wall up to the mouth of the

Tweed, crosses the Burn (and the modern road) west of the village.

Haydon Bridge (17). A small plain but pleasant little town situated on both banks of the broad South Tyne, which is crossed by a good six-arch bridge much repaired and partly re-done (the last time, some years ago, badly) since it was built in 1773. The severe late-eighteenth-century church has a pleasing tower. The old church, standing alone up the hillside to the north, where the medieval village lay, has a restored late Norman chancel, a fourteenth-century chantry chapel and a rebuilt nave, the Roman stones from some near-by camp being used in the rebuilding. The font is a re-used Roman altar.

John Martin, the painter, was born here, in 1789: as was his mad brother Jonathan who set fire to York Minster in 1829.

Langley Castle (1½ miles south-west) is one of the best and most impressive examples in the county of a fourteenth-century tower-house of the larger kind, though much rebuilt from a ruined condition by Cadwallader Bates, the historian, at the end of last century. It was owned by the Earls of Derwentwater and forfeited after the rising of 1715. On the

lovely road up from Haydon Bridge there is a massive memorial cross set up in 1883 to the earls who took part in both risings (1715 and 1745) and were beheaded at the Tower of London. The castle is now a school.

Staward Peel (4 miles south-west): a ruined fourteenth-century tower built partly of Roman stones, in a spectacular setting on the wooded and precipitous banks of the River Allen.

Healey (25). A hamlet in the wooded country between Riding Mill and the county boundary. The church neo-Norman of 1860.

Heddon-on-the-Wall (23). The Wall in the name is the Roman one, at the junction where the Military Road takes off from the Newcastle–Carlisle road on the outer skirts of the Tyneside conurbation. There is a good section of the foundations of it, with ditch and vallum, on the south side of the road to Newcastle. The church has some Anglo-Saxon bits, the chancel is Norman remodelled in the thirteenth century, the nave thirteenth century, extended and remodelled in the nineteenth.

Hedley-on-the-Hill (25). A nonde-

HAYDON BRIDGE

Nr. THROPTON, Coquetdale, and Long Crag. HEPPLE is to the left of the picture

script village high up with an enormous panorama over the Tyne valley and beyond, with Cheviot topping the view, 40 miles away.

Hepple (19). A scattered hamlet with the shell of a fourteenth-century peel-tower attached to farm buildings on the side of the road. There are wide and wild views over sweeping moorland. A small simple church of 1897 replaced one on another site destroyed long before by the Scots.

Witchy Neuk Camp, on the top of Swindon Hill to the south, with a great view over the Coquet valley, is one of many earthworks in the vicinity.

Hexham (18). A town with a tempestuous history. It was ravaged and sacked by the Danes in 876, and had a particularly bad patch in the fourteenth century when it was burned and pillaged by the Scots half a dozen times in fifty years. It has had other bad times too, some of them recent. In the 1930s the red rump of a cinema was allowed to rear itself up and almost block out the Abbey from the places where it had been seen for a thousand years dominating the skyline of the clustering town on the hill: and an enormous works with high buildings and erections that have been built in the last few years on the north bank of the river just to the east of the town does not improve its hitherto fine landscape setting. But in spite of all disasters past and present it remains a pleasant and interesting place.

Until 1572 the town, and an area round about, was a "regality" of the Archbishop of York under the name of Hexhamshire—a kind of minor Palatinate where the archbishops exercised an almost royal power.

The main building is, of course, the Abbey or Priory Church. It was founded about 673: and parts of the first building remain in the small crypt, built at least partly, perhaps wholly, of Roman stones. But the building as we see it today is essentially of two widely separated periods, 1180–1250 and 1850–1910. The chancel and transepts, Transitional and Early English (beginning about 1180), are extremely fine and are generally regarded as outstanding of their kind. The east front, facing the market place, is dull and undistinguished, being one of Dobson's less successful designs (1858). And the nave, having remained in ruins since it was

85

destroyed by the Scots, was lifelessly designed anew by Temple Moore in 1908, its hard white stone contrasting harshly with the warm-coloured stone of the older parts. As a result of all this the church has a very patched-up look inside and out. Nevertheless, its fine parts are very fine indeed. So are its furnishings and monuments. The monks' Night Stair, one of the most monumental stairways in England, with its great flight of much-worn steps, has a moving quality of grandeur about it. The late-fifteenth-century woodwork of the rood screen and pulpitum, the earlier misericords to the choir stalls, the exquisitely delicate screens to the two chantries, and the various fifteenth-century painted panels, would be rich anywhere, let alone in a county where such things are uncommon. The extraordinarily virile and powerful carvings which some unknown Tudor genius made for the Leschman Chantry must be among the finest of their kind in the country (though they are very difficult to see). And there are other monuments and furnishings of great interest, among them the Roman memorial stone, showing a Roman horseman trampling a naked Briton; the frith-stool, a stone chair probably of the seventh or eighth century, one of the only two pre-Conquest episcopal thrones in the country; and various tombs and effigies.

Facing the Abbey across the market place (which has an attractive colonnaded market building of 1766) is the Moot Hall or Court House, a massive tower built before 1415. Beyond the gateway is the great ancient prison (1330); and, beyond that again, the old Grammar School (parts seventeenth century). There are good, mostly Georgian, buildings in the Market Place, Fore Street, Hencotes, Priestpopple, Battle Hill, Orchard Place, St Mary's Chare and Quatre Bras. And there is a charming little park, The Seal, with a pretty cast-iron bandstand, near the Abbey.

The long nine-arched bridge over the Tyne was designed by Robert Mylne in 1785.

Hexham was the scene of the tragic

HEXHAM Abbey

HEXHAM Abbey:
The North transept
from the Night Stair

riot in 1761, when soldiers fired on a crowd protesting against the method of being called to the militia, 50 people being killed and some 300 injured.

Devil's Water. On the banks of this tributary of the Tyne (2½ miles southeast) the Battle of Hexham was fought in 1463. And it was in Dipton Woods nearby that Queen Margaret and her infant son had their adventurous escape from robbers, and hid in a cave before they escaped to Scotland.

St John's Lee (1 mile north) is a nineteenth-century church with a prominent spire, standing alone on a high wooded bluff.

Holy Island (or Lindisfarne) (6). Truly called, for in spite of stormy years, what with the Danes and the Scots, it was (with Canterbury) the cradle of Christianity in England. Aidan, the missionary from Iona, arrived here at the invitation of Oswald, King of Northumbria, in 635; and from then the light of Christian civilization began slowly to irradiate northern England.

The island is about 3½ miles long and about a mile broad at the widest. Most of the interest is centred at the southern extremity (the northern part, The Snook, being mostly sand dune and bent grass). Here are the ruins of the Priory, the village, the harbour, the castle, and a farm or two. The village, which is a substantial place with a little square, is a bit untidy, but has true island–village character. The dark red ruins of the Priory which succeeded the earlier Celtic cathedral church in the late eleventh century have great nobility: and in one striking view they very picturesquely frame the harbour and the castle beyond, rising out of its precipitous pinnacle of rock. The thir-

87

teenth-century village church has a curious almost eastern internal effect in a mixture of pink and white stone, and has an attractive line in wall tablets. The excitingly-sited small castle was built about 1500, had a garrison until the middle of last century, and at the beginning of this was restored by Sir Edwin Lutyens. It is now owned by the National Trust. Looking back from the island, beyond the sea and the sands and the gulls, one sees the woods and fields of the mainland rising up towards the Kyloes in the centre, with Cheviot and Hedgehope peeping up behind; to the right the high keep of the otherwise demolished Haggerstone Castle among trees; and, on the left, the great hump of Bamburgh Castle jutting into the sea, six miles away.

Access to the island (which used to be by a three-mile crossing of wet sand with the remains of abandoned cars lying deep sunk in the sand like the bones of camels in the desert, where one either rather dangerously walked or was driven by islanders in battered old Fords with the sea lapping on the floorboards), is now over a causeway, 3½ miles long, at shore level, where you can drive your own car—but still only when the tide permits.

Holystone (7). A hamlet on the edge of the heather, with a small bare pitch-piney chapel-church of 1848, where once there was an Augustinian Nunnery (founded before 1124). All signs of the Nunnery, which was often despoiled and its inhabitants molested by Scottish marauders, have now disappeared. St Paulinus is said to have baptized 3,000 converts in a single day at the Lady Well, a pool in a grove of trees now owned by the National Trust. A little westward at

HEXHAM

the farm called Campville is a primitive earthwork: and at Dove Crag there is a little waterfall, near which is Rob Roy's Cave which legend (and Sir Walter Scott) associated with the famous Scottish outlaw.

Horncliffe (1). A quiet village on a bluff above the wooded banks of the Tweed, with a surprising and beautiful bridge for the least used of the four roads crossing the river into Scotland. The bridge, the Union Bridge, which is over 140 yards long, and was the first suspension bridge to be built in Britain (1820), was designed by Sir Samuel Brown, a captain in the Royal Navy. It makes the most charming and graceful of all the crossings into Scotland.

Horsley (22). A straggling village which traffic rushes through on the Newcastle–Carlisle road, with spoiled views over the Tyne valley. It has an attractive inn dating from 1718: and a house dated 1700 but of a much earlier type.

Housesteads (14). With Chesters this is the most systematically explored Roman fort on the Wall, and the opposite of Chesters in situation, being wild and frontier-like, instead of softly situated in a park. From the main road the approach is up a southward facing slope, with extensive vestiges of terraces. There is a museum on the site.

Howick (9). A small, formal estate village approached on the south by tree-arched roads. The coast here is exceptionally fine, with the black basalt cliffs of Cullernose Point, and a sandy little bay at the mouth of the burn. Howick Hall (long associated with the Grey family among whom was Earl Grey of the Reform Bill fame) is a building from many hands. Designed by William Newton in 1782, altered by Wyatt in 1809, it was remodelled inside by Sir Herbert Baker (1928) after a disastrous fire. The church, which stands on the edge of a ravine, was built in 1746 and re-fashioned in Norman in 1849. There is a circular earthwork on Camp Hill, east of the Hall.

Humshaugh (15). A medium-large village, with cottage gardens behind stone walls, in fine country among

trees; another example, among many in England, of a village transferred to a new position from too close proximity to manorial windows. The old village lay about Haughton Castle, but when the demesne was landscaped, it was moved here out of sight. The church dates from 1818. Beside the river is a disused paper mill, built in 1788 and used by William Pitt in 1793 to forge French banknotes for use in an unsuccessful expedition to Flanders.

Haughton Castle (1 mile north) is a fine tower-house of the larger kind, in a lovely situation. Begun in the thirteenth century, it was mainly fourteenth-century construction, remained little more than a shell after partial destruction by raiders in 1542, and was restored, possibly by Dobson, and certainly by Salvin, in 1876. It is best seen from the opposite bank of the river, at Barrasford.

Ilderton (5–8). A few cottages and a church on a low hill, with Hedgehope and Cheviot in the background. The church was burned by the Scots about 1300; in 1715 the only part that was usable was the nave, roofed with turf; and when it was rebuilt later in that century, all that remained of the earlier church were the lower parts of the tower. In the churchyard is the mausoleum of the Rodham family, 1795. Rodham Hall (1 mile south) is an eighteenth-century mansion in dark grey stone. There are camp sites below Dod Hill and on the ridge of Roseden Edge.

Ingoe (22). A hamlet on an elevated setting. An eighteenth-century Hall. A 6-foot-high standing stone near a tumulus; and hut circles near by. Bronze Age relics were discovered here in 1860.

Ingram (8). A hall, a church, a farm and a few cottages well into the hills, with the road continuing westward for a few miles up the glen of the Breamish till it peters out near the 50-foot waterfall of Linhope Spout. The church standing beside the river is substantially Norman and thirteenth century, with chancel and aisles of the nineteenth.

On the higher points up the glen and up that of the tributary Shank Burn, there are at least twenty prehistoric camp sites. On Ingram Hill,

HOLY ISLAND
View from the Castle
The Castle
The Priory and the Castle

to the south, there is a cluster of round barrows and the relics of an early village, with the remains of its enclosing wall still to be seen. Farther up the valley, at Greaves Ash, 900 feet above sea level, are the striking remains of one of the largest of Northumberland's prehistoric villages on a site of 20 acres, with the vestiges of double walls and traces of hut-circles.

Kielder (10). Three and a half miles below the Border at Deadwater, at the junction of the North Tyne and Kielder Burn. Here in an attractive setting is planned one of the main villages of the Forestry Commission; but it has been left less than a third-finished. Kielder Castle standing above the village, was the eighteenth-century shooting box of the Dukes of Northumberland. It is now a club-house of the village.

This, and all the valley of the North Tyne, was a very wild part of the Border. Sir Walter Scott reported that he had been told by the 2nd Duke that when he visited Kielder in 1765, "the women had no other dress than a bed-gown and a petticoat. The men were savage and could hardly be brought to rise from the heather either from sullenness or from fear. They sang a wild tune. . . . The females sang, the men danced round and at a certain part of the tune they drew their dirks which they always wore." There are wild tales of Kielder and the rest of the valley too numerous to mention. And prehistoric and other remains too numerous to detail. A little south of the Border at Bells near Deadwater, there was, in 1715, "a mean village where are the ruins of an old chapel" in which the wardens of the English and Scottish Marches used to meet for consultations on peace. It has all disappeared, and so has the near-by castle of Kirshope; but a cairn in the old graveyard marks the grave of the Cout (Strong Man) of Kielder, who was closely associated with the landmark called the Kielder Stone, half in Scotland

and half in England. About Kielder there are at least seven contour forts, and traces of primitive dwellings at seven other places.

From *Peel Fell* (1,975 feet) there is a magnificent view on a clear day: westward, the Lake District hills, the Solway, and the Kirkcudbright and Wigtown fells; north, bumpy Scotland; north-east, the great hump of Cheviot; east, the North Sea. It is one of the few points whence you can see the sea on both sides of England.

Killingworth (24). A new town for a population of 20,000, started in 1963, on 760 acres of derelict colliery land surrounding an old mining village—an energetic and praiseworthy enterprise undertaken by the County Council, and not, as with most new towns, by national government agency. Interesting modern housing and industrial buildings, including the fine Norgas House (architects, Ryder and Yates), situated beside a lake constructed as a storm-water reservoir as part of the new town development.

It was at Killingworth, while living there and working as "brakesman", that George Stephenson designed and built his first railway engine, the *Blucher*, which first ran in 1814; and, ten years later, designed his *Locomotion No. 1* for the Darlington and Stockton Railway, the first public railway in the world.

Kirkharle (22). A hamlet among fields and woods in the vale of the Wansbeck; the birthplace, in 1715, of Lancelot (Capability) Brown, the landscape architect who did more than anyone else to create the great country parks of England. There is a good little fourteenth-century church, with a stone inscribed to a Richard Lorraine who in 1738 "Dyed a batchelor . . . walking in a green field near London"—an evocative phrase to find in these distant and remote parts.

Littleharle Tower (¾ mile north) is a Victorian mansion incorporating the shell of a medieval peel.

Kirkhaugh (16). A solitary nineteenth-century church with a slender needle-like spire in a romantic situation among mountainous country, on the extreme south-west edge of the county. There are two Bronze Age barrows of about 1000 B.C. which, until they were excavated in 1935, were thought to be mining dumps.

Whiteley Castle (1 mile south) is a Roman fort whose old name is not known. It covers nine acres, in a commanding position, and has four ramparts on three sides and no fewer than six on the other.

Kirkheaton (22). A forlorn-looking dead-end hamlet round a green. The

Farm near HORNCLIFFE. The 'factory' chimney is a common feature

KILLINGWORTH. Above: *Norgas House;* below: *Housing*

church was built in 1753. The Hall is late seventeenth century and incorporates some scanty remains of a medieval tower-house.

Kirknewton (4). A small village under the hills near the Border. The church, unsympathetically restored by Dobson about 1860, has a remarkable acutely-vaulted chancel and transept, the vaulting beginning about 3 feet from the ground; also a rude twelfth-century carving to the north of the chancel arch depicting the Presentation of the Magi, with the Wise Men wearing kilts. Josephine Butler, the Victorian social reformer, born at

Milfield nearby, is buried in the churchyard. There are earthworks on Gregory's Hill and West Hill.

North-westward the road runs to Kirk Yetholme, a famous gypsy "capital" just over the Border. From this road, three-quarters of a mile west of Kirknewton, a track winds up College Burn right into the hills, with Cheviot straight ahead, passing through the hamlet of Hethpool, where are the ruins of a fourteenth-century tower.

A little to the north of the hamlet of *Yeavering* (1½ miles east), on the banks of the River Glen, is *Coupland Castle,* one of the few castles fortified

(about 1619) after the Union with Scotland. Yeavering itself is the *Adgehrin* described by Bede as the summer residence of the Saxon king, Edwin, in the seventh century. Between the hamlet and Kirknewton, under Yeavering Bell, is a battle stone commemorating a victory, in 1415, of a small Northumbrian army over a much bigger Scottish one. The prominent obelisk at Lanton in the neighbourhood is a private memorial erected in 1829.

Yeavering Bell (2 miles south-east) is a bold hill of no great height (1,182 feet) but, after Hedgehope and Peel Fell, is one of the most reward-

93

Kilns near LONG HOUGHTON

ing climbs in the county, with great views over the valleys of the Till and the Tweed to the north, the Chatton hills to the east, with Cheviot and a tumble of other hills to the west and south. On the summit is one of the largest prehistoric camps or forts in the county, a most impressive sight, with the stones of the walls strewn about in the circle of the ramparts.

Kirkwhelpington (15). A village built round a churchyard, just off the main Carter Bar road, where the green lowland country changes to moor that stretches on uninterruptedly to Scotland. The long aisleless church is thirteenth century. There are more than a dozen camps and earthworks, probably Romano-British, in the locality, including Great Wanny, at 1,000 feet.

Knaresdale (16). The map shows this in bold type, but it should be in minute italics. It doesn't exist as a

place but the approaches to it are magnificent. There is a little church of 1838, and a seventeenth-century Hall.

Kyloe (5). Two hamlets, East and West, a mile apart. The church is at West Kyloe, prominent on a hill and with fine views of a great expanse of coast and sea: the tower (rebuilt Norman) is of 1792, and there is an apsidal chancel of 1862. East Kyloe has a ruined peel standing beside a farmhouse. Bronze Age burial relics were found in a quarry in 1927.

The Kyloe Hills, of no very great height (600 feet), craggy, with bracken, heather and plantations, give immense coastal and sea views: and on one of the strongest positions there is double-ramparted early earthwork.

Grizzy's Clump, a walled group of trees in a field by the side of the Great North Road, two miles south, was the scene of a romantic episode

in 1685 when Grizel Cochrane, dressed as a man, held up the mail coach and seized the death warrant against her father (or brother?) who had been sentenced for implication in the rising against James II, so delaying the execution and ultimately securing his release.

Lambley (16). A hamlet by the wooded banks of the South Tyne: a little nineteenth-century church and a handsome stone railway viaduct.

Lesbury (9). A tidy nineteenth-century stone-built village, with a simply and decently rebuilt church, a fine medieval bridge and a good nineteenth-century railway viaduct. There are many curious radar structures on the road to the north.

Lilburn (5). More a few scattered buildings and a proud association (with the family of Collingwood) than a place. A ruined early-Norman

North-facing hills near KIRKNEWTON

chapel: a ruined fourteenth-century tower: a house (Milburn Tower) by Dobson, 1828, and later.

Longframlington (20). An ordinary largish village with plain ashlar houses, in an attractive setting, where the moors begin. A little church, with late Norman bits, a fine chancel arch, and a curiously oriental-looking bell-turret.

Weldon Bridge (1½ miles south) is a graceful five-arched structure of 1744, with a well-known fishing inn alongside.

Longhirst (20). A well-kept estate village of pleasant ashlar houses, in a well-wooded bit of the coastal plain north-east of Morpeth. A church of 1876 by Sir Arthur Blomfield; and a Hall of Dobson's best period about 1828.

Longhorsley (20). A straggling un-distinguished village, with a very good small tower-house and a church of 1783 standing by a burn away from the village.

Long Houghton (9). An ordinary vil-lage with a good deal of modern housing, a bit back from the sea. The church, with a square and squat Norman tower, has a very primitive-looking interior with rough early Norman arches to the chancel and tower; but a lot of it was over-restored in 1873.

Little Houghton Tower (1 mile north-west) is a partly medieval tower, partly seventeenth-century house and partly eighteenth.

Lowick (5). A village on the Roman Road that runs southward from Tweedmouth. The church was built in 1794, medievalized forty years later and extended in 1887.

Matfen (23). A small village among trees, with a stream along one side of the green, and cottage gardens run-ning down to it. The mid-nineteenth-century church has a spire unusual in these parts. The big Hall, in a well-wooded park, is by Rickman, 1830. There is a large standing stone, the Stob Stone, 7 feet high, with cup-and-ring markings, to the south.

The clock tower at MORPETH

Meldon (23). Only one or two cottages, a humble little thirteenth-century church, and an imposing ashlar-faced house by Dobson, 1832.

Mitford (23). Scattered cottages, castle ruins on a steep knoll, ruins of a Carolean manor house, and eighteenth-century Hall, a Norman, thirteenth-, fourteenth- and nineteenth-century church with a spire—all romantically situated on a quiet wooded reach of the Wansbeck a little west of Morpeth.

Morpeth (20–23). Though near the coalfield, and to some extent a market town for the western part of it, Morpeth retains something of a corrupted country-town air. Above the chrome and vitriolite of the shopping streets some modest eighteenth-century brick façades remain: and, in the Market Place, the well-placed fifteenth-century tower or town steeple (an unusual structure in England), which still rings a curfew every evening at 8 o'clock, gives the centre some character. So must Vanbrugh's Town Hall have done before the fire of 1869 which necessitated its rebuilding; but it is no very great shakes now. And the use of the part thirteenth-century, part eighteenth-century church at the other end of the main street as a ladies' lavatory, a butcher's shop and a mineral water factory is not very civilized. But just off the centre there are pleasant buildings in Newgate, Oldgate, Cottingwood Lane and St James's Terraces. And St James' Church (1846, by Benjamin Ferrey) with a screen of columns and arches to the street and an avenue of trees leading to it, has a grand interior in lofty nineteenth-century Norman. Collingwood House, in Oldgate, was the home of Admiral Collingwood who was Nelson's deputy at Trafalgar and took command of the battle after Nelson received his fatal wound.

The large, fine parish church is well out of the town centre, on the high ground to the south, beyond the handsome Telford (and/or Dobson?) bridge of 1831. It has a beautiful plain fourteenth-century interior, with some glass of that time. There is a little watch-house in the churchyard, built in 1831 to guard against body-snatchers (it was last used for

watching in 1912, when the suffragettes were active). Behind the church is the castle, with scanty ruins but impressive earthworks on a strong site overlooking the river and the town. Down the hill towards the bridge, the Court House, once part of the County prison and now now the police station, has an oppressively heavy gateway by Dobson (1822).

In the neighbourhood of the town the banks of the Wansbeck are pleasantly wooded; and in the town itself a steep stretch of banks has been converted into a park. Here, once a year, the Northumberland miners have their gala day, with fun and games, and beer and pies, and politics.

Newminster Abbey (1½ miles west, along the road to Mitford). The scanty ruins and excavated foundations of an early twelfth-century Cistercian monastery.

Netherton (8). A hamlet with modern stone houses and a modern school remote in a wide bowl surrounded by grassy hills.

Netherwitton (19–20). A small village in the sheltered valley of the River Font, with the Simonsides beyond. An old bridge of two arches; a Hall, well seen from the road, of about 1700, probably designed by Robert Trollope; an eighteenth-century church gothicized in 1886, with a bell-cote crowned by an obelisk; a disused late-eighteenth-century mill by the burn. One summer night in 1651, Cromwell camped with his army in the grounds of the manor house which preceded the present Hall.

Nunnykirk Hall (2 miles northwest) is one of Dobson's finest houses, built in 1825. In the garden there is the carved shaft of a ninth-century cross.

Newbiggin-by-the-Sea (21). A mining, fishing and holiday village, with a wide bay of sands bordered by low cliffs. Some pleasant houses facing the sea and the main street: a little square at the landing place. Otherwise poor in buildings, except for the church, rather gaunt with a tower that has a marked batter and a distinctive stumpy spire, which seems almost to stand in the sea, on a low bare headland. It is mainly thirteenth-

century, with the chancel from just after the turn of 1300. The spire is also fourteenth-century, one of only two such in the county, the other being at Warkworth.

Camps and cars and caravans by the shore near the church.

Newbrough (14). On the Roman road, Stanegate, which acted as a distributive road behind the Wall. There was a Roman fort here. In 1221 Henry III granted the establishment of a market, round which a "new town" grew up. Now it consists of a very nice eighteenth-century house, a nineteenth-century "Town Hall", and a few nineteenth-century houses and some new ones; as well as a little nineteenth-century church, a Hall by Dobson (1821), and the remains of a peel (Thornton Tower) in a farmyard. All well situated in the wooded Tyne Valley.

Newburn (23). A mining and industrial place linked now to Newcastle. The church, on a knoll above the main street, has an early Norman tower, the rest being Norman and nineteenth century. There are associations with George Stephenson who lived here for a time: and much longer ones with William Hedley, the designer of the locomotive Puffing Billy, now in the Science Museum at South Kensington.

Newcastle upon Tyne (23–26). Distinguished among English provincial cities for the quality of its architecture, Newcastle is the cultural and commercial centre of much of County Durham, and to some extent of Cumberland also, as well as of Northumberland. And it has the air of a genuine regional capital about it. Were it not for the existence of merely administrative boundaries (which in any case may soon disappear), its population should indeed be listed at something near 1,000,000, instead of 270,000, for the great spread of contiguous buildings down both banks of the Tyne really constitutes one large city.

Most parts of this conurbation (as town planners call such an agglomeration of contiguous towns), and

SURTEES HOUSE
Sandgate, Newcastle

96

great areas of Newcastle itself, are a solid concentration of dreary streets of drab little houses, as industrial towns are everywhere; but, unlike the central parts of most English cities, those of Newcastle have a striking civic character and architectural homogeneity. This is chiefly due to the genius and public spirit of Richard Grainger, its builder, and John Dobson, his architect. And the remarkable thing about this work is its date. There are as fine (indeed finer) examples of town planning in England—Bath, the London squares, Cheltenham, Brighton and other places: and Edinburgh New Town, as an example in Scotland. But *they* were built in the eighteenth century and first years of the nineteenth, when there was still a strong tradition of civic architecture in Britain. The centre of Newcastle was built later, towards the middle of the nineteenth century, when English town-building, under the curiously mixed influences of the Industrial Revolution and the Romantic Revival, had already begun its gloomy decline. Moreover, while the other examples of fine town planning, in Bath, Edinburgh and elsewhere, were for domestic quarters, this building in central Newcastle was from the beginning intended for commercial purposes, shops, offices and the like—a town centre from the start: the only one of its kind in England, and one of the few anywhere.

Richard Grainger was an entirely self-made man who started life as a jobbing carpenter. He made a large fortune out of his building work; but he had ideals for improving the city as well as making money, and he did remarkably courageous things to get the best effects, such as (to take a single example) pulling down a large comparatively new market building, and a theatre, so as to get the best line for Grey Street. John Dobson, his main architect, was the son of a local inn-keeper, born with a genius for design. With these two was joined the Town Clerk of the time, John Clayton.

This new town centre was built with extraordinary energy and rapidity

GREY STREET, Newcastle

in the course of five or six years (1835–40)—mostly on the grounds of a nunnery and a friary. Grey Street was the main street and is still the best (though it should be noted that the two buildings that are its most telling features, the Theatre Royal with its fine portico, and the Grey Monument, are not by Dobson, but by another architect, Benjamin Green). Among the other new streets were Grainger Street, Market Street, Clayton Street, Eldon Square, Nun Street, Nelson Street and Hood Street, besides the great covered markets, several shopping arcades and other features. They have all been blackened by a hundred years of soot (though many have recently been cleaned), many of the roof lines have been jagged and broken in places, and almost everywhere the ground storeys of the façades have been messed up by commerce: but in spite of this, these central streets still have a notable homogeneity and dignity (in contrast to the more normal jazzed-up squalor of city-centres, as it is seen in those parts of the centre of Newcastle itself, notably in Northumberland Street, which were outside the Grainger plan).

There are also fairly extensive

NEWCASTLE: Clayton Street
  (below) *Bentinck Terrace*
  (opposite) *Central Station*

quarters of decent domestic architecture north of the city centre, in Leazes Terrace (an early Grainger venture, with Thomas Oliver as architect; not improved as "desirable residential property" by the proximity of the United's football ground), and such little streets as St Thomas' Crescent near by; and in the handsome Jesmond Road terraces built in robust, rough-looking northern brickwork. There are other pleasant late-Georgian and early-Victorian quarters in other parts, such, for example, as Rye Hill (some of which had been going slummy until the Corporation organized their rehabilitation). Extensive parts of the city outside the central area, especially the wide locality of Elswick, off the Scotswood Road (much of it also by Grainger) are in course of rebuilding —inevitably, of course, with high towers and slabs of flats. Rebuilding was certainly very necessary. But less necessary, and indeed regrettable, has been the destruction here and there of attractive streets closer in— as in the University's destruction of the early nineteenth-century Eldon Place which would have maintained, within its enclave, a happy domestic foil to its oppressively massive buildings. And even more regrettable, indeed unforgivable, is the declared intention of the City Corporation (in 1967) to demolish Eldon Square, the fine large formal quadrangle of buildings which, ten years earlier in date, is second only in quality to Grey Street itself in the part it plays in the comprehensive Grainger-Dobson work which gives the city such distinction.

The older part of the city is mostly on the hillside that rises from the river quays: and it is overtopped by great bridges. It has a strong character of its own with massive blackened office blocks on narrow steep streets, and long steep-stepped cliff-side alleys between them, running down to views of ships and the river, though many of the alleys have long ago fallen into dereliction. Among the few old buildings that remain, there are, in Sandgate, one or two notable examples of seventeenth-century houses whose façades are more than

half glass. In the evenings and at weekends this part of the city is almost empty of people—except on Sunday mornings when there is a famous Petticoat-Lane-like market on the quayside.

Of the earliest history of the city there are naturally not many visible relics. Newcastle (then named *Pons Aelius*) was one of the forts on the Roman Wall: and there was a Roman bridge over the river where the Swing Bridge is now. Excavations have shown that the fort was on the ground now occupied by the Castle: but there is nothing of it to be seen today. Of the twelfth-century Castle the massive Norman keep remains (blackened with soot and surrounded by railway lines): and also the Black Gate which was originally the Castle's gatehouse. Both are museums, the Castle housing mixed antiquities and the Black Gate the most extensive collection of Roman inscribed and sculptured stones that there is in the country.

Of the medieval town walls dating from the middle of the thirteenth century (and which Leland described in 1540 as being of such "strength and magnificence" that "far passith all the wauls of the cities of England and most of the cities of Europe") there are still some lengths and some towers which survived the extensive destructions of the nineteenth century. The best stretch is westwards and then southwards from the junction of Newgate Street and Percy Street near St Andrew's Church; there is another section near Hanover Square; and there are two or three isolated towers standing elsewhere.

The city had a stirring medieval history, being several times assaulted and besieged by the Scots. It was again twice occupied by Scottish armies in the seventeenth-century Civil War, in which it played a considerable part, and of which there is a reminder on a bronze tablet in Market Street stating that "On this site formerly stood Anderson Place in which King Charles I was prisoner from 13th May 1646 to 3rd February 1647 during the Scottish occupation of the city,"—a further point of interest here being that it was in the extensive grounds of this same Anderson Place that Grainger undertook his great building operations.

The cathedral was St Nicholas' Parish Church until the new See of Northumberland was created in 1878. Externally it is not of very great importance, except for the remarkable and impressive "crown spire" (*c.* 1435) which stands above the tower with a delicate lantern supported on open arches (St Giles' Cathedral, Edinburgh, has a similar feature, but it was built half a century later). But internally the fourteenth-century church is impressive and has much beauty. The nave has a distinct slope down towards the chancel: there are some good furnishings, effigies and wall-tablets. Other old churches in the centre of the city are St John's, which stands, very battered-looking, at the foot of Grainger Street: and St Andrew's which stands in a churchyard at the head of Newgate Street. Among the great number of churches lying outside the city centre, St Ann's, along the sordid City Road, has a decent classical exterior (1812) and an elegant tower (architect, William Newton), Dobson's St Thomas' (1825) at Barras Bridge is externally hard and dull and ugly: and St Matthew's, Westgate Road (by R. J. Johnson, 1877–88) has a lofty light nave in dun-coloured stone, with an attractive east window and a very elegant later tower.

But the gem of all Newcastle churches is All Saints' in the old town, above the Quayside. It was designed in 1786 by David Stephenson (who was also responsible for a pre-Grainger piece of town planning in the building of Dean Street and Moseley Street). A parish church now almost without parishioners, it was recently threatened with demolition; but it has mercifully been spared, though its future use is still somewhat uncertain. Splendidly situated on the steep bankside, so that not even soot, old neglect and new squalor in its surroundings can wholly compromise it, its delicately-stepped classical spire rises majestically above the Newcastle sky-line; and its semi-circular interior is filled with some of the most exquisite wrought mahogany woodwork that proud craftsmen have ever created. It is probably the best individual classical building in Northumberland.

Among the other good buildings

are the Guildhall (partly by Robert Trollope, 1658); Customs House (1766, remodelled by Sidney Smirke, 1840); Trinity House and Chapel, in Broad Chare; the Theatre Royal; the extremely fine Central Station, designed by Dobson, 1846–50; and the Assembly Rooms (1776, by William Newton), in spite of the regrettable canopy that disfigures its entrance. And there are some notable engineering works, particularly the High Level Bridge (the earliest of the four high bridges that span the steep valley) which was built by Robert Stephenson in 1849, and was the first bridge in which cast-iron girders were used on anything like this scale.

The University, at Barras Bridge, sensibly retaining its near-central site instead of going to the suburbs, has grown enormous through the space

of a few years in a complex of massive buildings by various architects. The Town Hall, near by, is a great slab of a building with a Swedish-looking tower and a charming circular Council Chamber almost detached from the rest in the mode of a cathedral chapter-house (architect, George Kenyon). The Hancock Natural History Museum (John Wardle, 1878) is in the same locality; and the Municipal Museum of Science and Industry is a little to the north in Exhibition Park. The Laing Art Gallery, which among its fine collection has a substantial assemblage of Bewick engravings, is in New Bridge Street.

In its huge, bare Town Moor, Newcastle has a magnificent near-central open space. Jesmond Dene, in the eastern part of the city, is a very attractive piece of Victorian romantic landscaping—a long wooded

glen that was rescued from rubbish-dumping in 1883. And the sea is only eight miles away.

Newton-on-the-Moor (9). A small estate hamlet of 1885, built in stone and pantiles, with a distant view of the sea. The Hall is of 1772 with additions and alterations by Dobson in 1851.

Norham (1). One of the largest villages in the county, rather plain but with decent northern houses (some with a Scottish look) facing on to greens and a triangular central place with a nineteenth-century cross on a medieval base. At the east end the massive ruined castle keep (c. 1160, on the site of an earlier wooden castle of 1121) stands above trees on a site of great natural strength, dominating the village and the neighbourhood. Now preserved by the

NORHAM Church

Ministry of Public Building and Works, it had a stormy history, being several times besieged (twice by Bruce for long periods) and badly battered by the Scots before the Battle of Flodden. At the other end of the village in an enormous church-yard and on the site of an earlier church of 830, is the long flat-roofed-looking transeptless church. The pulpit, vicar's stall and organ screen are elaborately-carved seventeenth-century work from Durham Cathedral; and there is a fine monument of 1320 in the chancel.

The district round about is known as Norhamshire and was a detached part of the County Palatine of Durham until 1844. On the other side of the Tweed, Scotland begins in fine trees.

North Shields (24). Now part of the borough of Tynemouth, but once a separate town, it still has a few late-seventeenth-century brick houses and some formal streets and squares built in extension and improvement plans of the late eighteenth and early nineteenth centuries: but much has been demolished, and what remains is mostly now seedy and run-down. The Market Place or New Quay, Northumberland Square, Howard Street, Dockwray Square still retain some character: but there is a sad

blight over most of the rest. Christ Church, originally by Robert Trollope, c. 1660, was handsomely rebuilt in 1792: Holy Trinity, 1836, was by John Green: Roman Catholic St Cuthbert's by Robert Giles in 1821: and there are several Nonconformist Churches of the early-nineteenth-century rebuilding period, some of them no longer used for what they were. The Town Hall is an Eliza-bethan essay by Dobson (1844). Altogether the place has something of a forlorn air about it.

North Sunderland (6). Runs with Seahouses to make one village, much developed with bungalows. There is a church by Salvin (1834), and a Presbyterian Church of 1810. Some Bronze Age remains were found here in 1905.

Nunwick (14). At one time there was a village here, between the road and the river: but it has gone: and now there is only the Hall, a fine house of 1760 with alterations of 1829, standing in wooded grounds.

Ogle (23). A few cottages and modern bungalows—all rather forlorn-looking. Ogle Castle is a tower-house of the fourteenth century with fifteenth–sixteenth-century manor house added.

Old Bewick (8). A hamlet under a bracken-covered hill on the summit of which is a promontory fort of two horseshoe-shaped earthworks each with a double-rampart and ditch, with still another bank enclosing both. Hut circles, symbolically-marked stone blocks and Roman pottery were found here in 1933. There are wide views from the hill top. The small Norman church is among trees beside the Kirk Burn, near where it joins the River Breamish, which changes its name to the Till at the single-arched Bewick Bridge.

Otterburn (12). A substantial, scattered, rather characterless village in the bare wide valley of Redesdale on the Carter Bar road to Scotland: chiefly famous for the battle fought here in 1388 and celebrated in the Border Ballad which begins with the evocative lines:
It fell about the Lammas tide
When the muir men win their hay . . .
The church is by Dobson (1858): Otterburn Tower, with some eigh-teenth-century work and some bits of medieval masonry, is mostly Victorian: there is a large hotel; and the mill by the bridge is where

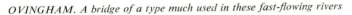
OVINGHAM. A bridge of a type much used in these fast-flowing rivers

the famous Otterburn tweeds are made. There are various camps about: Fawdon Hill with two ramparts 8 feet high and ditches; Coldwell Hill, with irregular circular fortifications 6 feet to 12 feet high; Greenchesters, with earthworks, in the fields overlooking the River Rede.

Ovingham (25). A pleasant riverside village now somewhat suburban for Newcastle. There are some old houses: the attractive mainly thirteenth-century church has a late-Saxon tower, some of its stones coming from the Roman Wall; the vicarage is part fourteenth century, part seventeenth and part nineteenth: there is a little stone packbridge over the Whittle Burn, above which, in the woods where that burn is joined by the Bogle Burn, a heap of overgrown stones marks the site of a castle, begun in 1271 but never finished; and there is a narrow iron bridge over the Tyne to Prudhoe.

Thomas Bewick, the famous engraver, was born across the river at Cherryburn and is buried in Ovingham churchyard.

Ovington (25), a mile west of Ovingham, is a mixed village on high ground.

Ponteland (23). Once rated a beauty spot, now extensive "garden suburbia". But the church with its sturdy Norman tower, fine thirteenth-century chancel, fourteenth and later additions, is a notable building, as is the manor house (now the Blackbird Inn), partly a fourteenth-century fortified house and mainly Tudor; while the rectory is an eighteenth-century brick house unusually gracious for Northumberland, and has in its garden the remains of a vicar's peel.

Prudhoe (25). On the hillside below the straggling mining and industrial half-town, and embowered and largely hidden in trees, is one of the best castles in the county, partly ruined but still inhabited. Strongly sited, with the steep fall to the Tyne on one side and a ravine on another, it has a free-standing twelfth-century

PRUDHOE Castle

108

Cragside, by Norman Shaw: ROTHBURY

keep (probably the oldest in Northumberland) some 65 feet high; a Norman - thirteenth - century gatehouse; and a mid-fourteenth-century barbican.

Rennington (9). A roadside hamlet of ordinary character, with a church of 1831–63.

Riding Mill (25). Mostly a "residential" village; but also a seventeenth-century manor house with additions of 1810; and a hotel of 1660.

Rochester (11). A hamlet on the Carter Bar road, with a good 1914–18 war memorial on the roadside.

High Rochester or *Bremenium* (½ mile north) is the site of an important Roman station splendidly situated on high ground with green rolling moors in every direction.

All over these hills towards Scotland, north and east of the Carter Bar road, there are camps and forts of various kinds early and late; the latter sometimes being mere groups of hutments, for after two thousand years the hills are still much occupied by soldiers; today with different weapons, for this, over to the springs of the Coquet and the Breamish, is

the training ground for artillerymen.

Rock (9). A nicely-built, grass-verged, estate-planned hamlet lying between main road and Hall gates, built about 1860, at the time when the little church was almost entirely rebuilt (only the Norman west doorway remaining) in a powerful "romanesque" style, and was given an enormous organ which must reverberate wonderfully if it is ever given its full blast. The Hall, now a youth hostel, is part sixteenth-century towerhouse, part Jacobean, part eighteenth century, part substantial remodelling by Dobson in 1819.

Rothbury (19). A small attractive hillside town, finely situated in the valley of the Coquet under wooded hills on the north, the pine-wooded heights of Cragside on the east, and the open Simonside hills on the south. It has nothing of particularly outstanding architectural character, but has good plain stone buildings, interesting levels, well-kept greens with fine trees, the whole making an altogether softer effect than is usual in Northumberland. It is sometimes over-popular for comfort in holiday months, but in its normal character is an important market

centre for the surrounding country in the rest of the year. The church, rebuilt (except for the thirteenth-century chancel) in 1850 is undistinguished in itself, but has a very distinguished font made of a carved shaft (part of a cross of about 800) and a bowl of 1664. There are a number of old and new large houses in the neighbourhood; and many prehistoric camps on the hills round about.

Cragside (1½ miles north-east). A mansion of 1870 by Norman Shaw in huge lofty romantic grounds which are open to the public (by car or on foot) during certain days of the week.

Cartington Castle (4 miles north-west). Splendidly situated high up on Lorbottle Crags at the edge of the moors: a picturesque ruin of fourteenth-century and later building.

Whitton (1½ miles south). A fourteenth-century tower-house, part of a later house that is now a children's home with *Sharp's Folly*, a 50-feet-tall outlook tower of 1720, on high ground nearby. Nearby, too, is *Whitton Grange*, a good building of 1920, by Mauchlen and Weightman.

Great Tosson (2 miles south-west). Below Simonside (1409 feet) the 30-feet-high ruin of an early peel. At

the next near hamlet of Newtown (2 miles south-west) is an empty mill where once-famous tweeds were made, the secret of their making dying out with the two brothers who managed it.

Among the camps and earthworks are—Old Rothbury, with traces of a double ditch and rampart: Lordenshaws, 880 feet high, ditches and double banks up to 6 feet high: Tosson Burgh, on the top of Tosson at 1,447 feet: Westhill Camp, parts of inner and outer ramparts rising to 6 feet. Also barrows and standing stones at among other sites, Debdon Moor, Whitefield Moor, Garleigh Moor.

Ryal (22). An upland hamlet of a short row of stone houses, a little rebuilt church; and, to the south, on the green hill of Grindstone Law, a round contour fort with mound and ditch.

Seahouses (6). The old part is an attractive fishing village with a pier: there are sandhills (some owned by the National Trust), and splendid sands; and this is the place from which to make the trip to the Farne Islands, standing three miles out to sea. But the old character is almost submerged now by too many villas and bungalows, joining up with North Sunderland. There is a good modern Methodist Chapel of the 30s by Mauchlen and Weightman.

Seaton Delaval (24). A long straggling colliery village in the flat featureless coalfield of the south-eastern corner of the county.

About two miles to the east, down a mile-long avenue, and admirably seen over a ha-ha from the public road which passes close by, is the great Hall of the Delavals. It was the last (and one of the best) of Vanbrugh's great houses, being begun 1720 and completed in 1729, after his death. Here the Delaval family lived a wild, extravagant life: and the house itself had a wild, extravagant history. A disastrous fire destroyed the west wing in 1752, but it was rebuilt to the original design. In 1822 there was a second and bigger blaze which left it more or less a ruin.

The Stables, SEATON DELAVAL Hall

Patched up in the 1860s, it went back again, until recently, to dereliction, untenanted, a fire-licked roofless shell. Now it has been recovered again, and one can only hope it will have better luck this time. It has a haunting magnificence in the ruined countryside about.

In the grounds of the house is a large orangery, and a mausoleum of 1766, where lies the last of the Delavals, John, who died, aged 20, in 1775, "as a result of being kicked in a vital organ by a laundrymaid to whom he was paying his addresses".

The small church has extensive Norman and early fourteenth-century work.

Seaton Sluice. Farther down the road is the harbour constructed by the Delavals. In the seventeenth century they built a weir across the Seaton Burn, with a sluice to scour the harbour—hence the name. Next century they cut a wide, deep channel through hundreds of feet of solid rock to make another entrance. For two hundred years the port flourished, at one time having its own fleet of twenty-two sailing ships. Last century it fell into decay, the harbour mouth blocked by the ruins of former walls and jetties. Now it has been sufficiently recovered to provide anchorage for yachts and small craft.

The old village of Seaton Sluice must have been pleasant as well as busy. The modern extensions are neither.

Shilbottle (9). A long straggling village, with a pit, an outlier of the coalfield. The big church was rebuilt, by William Hicks, in 1884, but has Norman features. The vicarage incorporates a fourteenth-century tower, a Vicar's Peel.

Shotley (25). A scattered place on the Northumberland side of the River Derwent with the larger Shotley Bridge on the Durham side. Two churches: one, St Andrew, built in 1768 and remodelled in 1892, stands alone except for an archaic-looking and domed mausoleum of *c.* 1750; the other, St John's, of 1835, has a chancel apse of 1903 and a good modern window by L. C. Evatts.

Simonburn (14). A small quiet hamlet about a square green, back from the main road, among woods and

Seaton Sluice, SEATON DELAVAL

SEATON DELAVAL Hall, The central block before the recent extensive restoration

park scenery; described in the Survey of 1541 as "a strong town in a very strong ground". The good parish church, mostly rebuilt (by Salvin) about 1860, has a floor sloping down to the altar; the rectory of 1725 looks Vanbrughesque: and there are scanty ruins of a thirteenth-century castle on a romantic site down a lane half-a-mile to the west. The ruin of the castle is said to have resulted more from villagers than from border warfare, for there was an old tradition of treasure buried in the walls.

The parish of Simonburn once stretched up to the Scottish border, 30 miles away.

Slaley (18). A usual village in the remote-seeming unusual countryside about Devil's Water where it flows down to meet the Tyne near Corbridge. A church of 1832.

Stamfordham (22). A medium-large village, once one of the best in Northumberland; originally a small market town. Until the 1960s it was rather bare and very earthy-looking, mostly a long row of varied eighteenth-century houses in colour-wash, stone and brick, facing on to a sloping green with a little market building (1735) and a village lock-up on it. Many of the houses have since then been rebuilt in an over-architected style and fanciful materials, and the character has been changed. The impressive thirteenth-century, but over-restored church, on a slight rise at the west end of the village, has effigies and monuments, including a rude carving of the Crucifixion and a Renaissance tomb of 1623. The vicarage is partly Tudor partly eighteenth century. There are some villas towards the east, fortunately hidden from the main village.

Stannington (23). An estate hamlet adjoining the Great North Road, with a large-towered church mainly of 1871, by R. J. Johnson, but containing some bits of Norman work and, in the vestry window, some fourteenth-century glass.

Blagdon Hall, the local great house, was built about 1734–40, altered by

James Wyatt in 1778–91, added to by Joseph Bonomi of Newcastle in 1826–30, burned in 1944, and re-duced and restored by Robert Lutyens in 1949. The gardens were remodelled by Sir Edwin Lutyens in 1938. The octagonal lodges on the main road are by Wyatt (1786), with Ridley bulls on the gateposts. The stables are also by Wyatt. There is a conduit cross, designed by David Stephenson and removed from New-castle in 1807, near the north lodge: also removed into the grounds from Newcastle is a temple of 1783 by William Newton.

Stonehaugh (14). Four miles west of Wark on a plateau by the Warks Burn, the first part of a large new village for the Forestry Commission. Along one side the river flows through a gorge like a small canyon. The village was planned to have a population of about 800 but has been left a quarter finished.

Thockrington (22). Away from any-where, high up and solitary and little more than a church, a farm and some old trees. The church is Norman with a thirteenth-century east end.

There are lakes about here. Colt Crag and Hallington are reservoirs: but Sweethope Lough, 2 miles north-wards over the hills is a more natural lake, at the source of the Wansbeck. There are also crags frequented by climbers. And camps that once were frequented by Romans and earlier Britons.

Thropton (8). A good though strag-gling village under the Simonsides, with a bastel-house, and a good modest little Roman Catholic church of 1811–42.

Tillmouth and **Twizell** (4). Neither of them even a hamlet, but they run more or less together. *Tillmouth* is where the Till joins the Tweed. There is a nineteenth-century hotel in a park, a ruined eighteenth-century chapel, a ferry into Scotland. *Twizell* is a fine fifteenth-century bridge in a lovely setting, a single span of 90 feet flying high across the wooded glen of the Till: and, beside that, the ivy-covered ruin of Twizell Castle is not a relic of Border defence but a monster folly begun about 1770 and never finished.

Tweedmouth (2). With Spittal, cross-Tweed suburbs of Berwick. Common-place enough in themselves, they occasionally give splendid views of the fine town across the water and its three bridges. Tweedmouth church was built in 1783 and gothicized in 1866.

Tynemouth (24). Joined now with North Shields, Cullercoats and Whit-ley Bay, the town of Tynemouth proper, in spite of being a monastic settlement since the early seventh century, dates only from about 1800. It was then that its cliff-top terraces began to be built and it began to be-come a fashionable watering place attracting numbers of distinguished visitors. Many of these terraces, and later ones, survive, in Front Street, Dawson Square, Allendale Place, Newcastle Terrace, Bath Terrace and others—plain stately terraces with nice balconies and doorways. Most of the rest of the town is ordinary un-distinguished later streets. The sea-front has grassy cliffs and is high, breezy and bracing. Below are fine sands. And dominating all are the impressive ruins of the Priory and castle on the jutting headland that guards the mouth of the Tyne.

The Priory, founded in the seventh century, had a difficult beginning. It was ravaged by the Danes in 800, destroyed in 865, ravaged again in 870. Before the refounding and re-building (*c.* 1090) it seems to have been abandoned for a century. The remains now are of eleventh-and twelfth-century work, all mixed up with those of the fourteenth-century castle ruins, for priory and castle seem all to have been more or less one here. The nave of the church con-tinued in use for local inhabitants until Christ Church at North Shields was built about 1660, and the grave-yard was in use until modern times.

Among other buildings in the town are the 1841 church of The Holy Saviour (John and Benjamin Green): a large monument to Admiral Collingwood by Dobson (1847), with a 23-foot statue by Lough on a 50-foot-high pedestal; the Tyne Master Mariners Asylum (by the Greens: 1837): and a streaky gothic clock-tower of 1861.

From the height of the headland you can look down on to the immense breakwaters that form the protected mouth of the Tyne.

Ulgham (20): pronounced Uffm. An old hamlet accumulating modern houses, by the infant trickle of the small River Lyne. Markets are said to have been held here when there was plague in Morpeth: and there are remains of an old market cross by the roadside. The little church of 1862, unremarkable in itself, has a somewhat remarkable piece of carv-ing in a kind of child's art—Norman, of a woman with two birds over her shoulder and a man on an Uffington-looking horse beside her.

Wall (15). An attractive roadside vil-lage, a church of 1896 and, at the other end, a good hotel. There is a good exposed stretch of the Roman Wall at Brunton Bank, ½ mile north: and farther on, by the side road up to the Military Road and standing back from that, is *St Oswald's* chapel, built in 1737, gothicized in 1887. Out in a field, surrounded by trees, it commemorates the Battle of Heaven-field where, in 635, Oswald defeated the British king Cadwallon and so won Northumbria for Christianity.

Wallsend (24). Once a fort (Sege-dunum) at the eastern end of the Roman Wall, now a colliery engin-eering and shipbuilding town, one of the sombre links in the Tyneside conurbation. But here, if men did not know how to build a town, they built and still build splendid machines. The first noble *Mauretania* was built here in 1907, and many other fine ships and many wonders of engineering have been born in this grim place.

Warden (15). A hamlet among trees at the junction of the north and south parts of the Tyne. A hall, a few cottages, and a church with a tall Saxon tower. On High Warden Hill, to the north, there is a large Iron Age earthwork with ramparts of stone from the Prudham quarries near by, where stone is still worked.

Wark-on-Tweed (4). An undistin-guished hamlet of little interest today, but in medieval times one of the great fortresses of the Border, subject to numerous sieges, captures and recaptures. Not a stone of the castle

SEATON DELAVAL HALL: the North front

remains standing; but the big mound on which it stood, and other earthworks, can be seen.

Wark-on-Tyne (14). Capital of North Tynedale in the twelfth and thirteenth centuries, when for a time this was part of Scotland: now a medium-sized village, situated on a beautiful reach of river, still with something of a small town air about its few plain-fronted streets and its quadrangle of houses facing a green. The church is of 1814–18: and there are the remains of the mound of a Norman motte-and-bailey.

Chipchase Castle (1½ miles south-east) is one of the best examples of a fourteenth-century tower-house in the county, with a Jacobean manor-house added in 1621. By the castle is a mid-eighteenth-century chapel in which are fine box-pews and double-decker octagonal pulpit.

SEATON DELAVAL: the South front

Warkworth (9). A grey striking little town encompassed on three sides by a loop of the Coquet, approached from the north, before the fine new bridge of the 1960s was built near by, over a narrow medieval bridge and through an arch that is a remnant of the old gatehouse that guarded it— one of the few fortified bridges in England. From the bridge and the distinguished early eighteenth-century house which stands by it, a short street with good plain houses splays to the small market place and from there the wide main street rises steeply, raked and dominated by the great castle at the top—the most impressive ruin in a county of fine ruins, and one of the most tremendous street views in Britain. The finest view of all is back a little towards the porch of the church, where the castle seems to take on an even more terrific presence. Up the main street, as in the market place

also, the stone buildings are again of good plain northern vernacular of somewhat stern aspect suitable to the castle beyond (though that itself is of a softer lighter colour): and the sternness has been unnecessarily emphasized by the paving over in tinted tarmac of the bits of grass and cobble that once enlivened the street floor (why do Councils do this kind of thing? and why did they authorize the red-brick garage which is so out of character?). At the top of the hill the road sweeps round the castle and out of the little town (though unfortunately on to a string of singularly inappropriate villas which mar the approach from the south and the setting of the castle there).

The downhill view of the main street from the castle is nothing like so impressive as the upward view, and the church is off centre in it: but it is still the view of a good town,

Main line viaduct
STANNINGTON VALE
TWIZELL Bridge

and the church itself is almost as rewarding as the castle is. It is one of the largest in the county and is something of a summary of English ecclesiastical building: the main body Norman, the tower late-twelfth or early-thirteenth century, the spire fourteenth and the porch fifteenth century. The nave is unusually long —the longest in Northumberland: the chancel is one of the few twelfth-century vaulted chancels in English parish churches. There is a fine figure of a knight of about 1330 on a seventeenth-century stone tomb. The room above the church was formerly the local school.

The castle was begun in the twelfth century and a good deal of the present structure dates from that time; but its main building period

STAMFORDHAM

was the late-fourteenth and early-fifteenth centuries, when its most dominant feature, the great keep (which is of unusual beauty) was built, and when the beginnings of a domestic character, such as is noticeable in the window openings, were creeping into castle building. The Percy lion figures sculptured on the walls. From the castle and the paths beside it on the west you look down the steep wooded glen of the Coquet, a lovely scene—great hanging woods, partly beech on one side; the still river below; and green haugh and hillside beyond; while, from below, the castle rises splendid on its

great height at the end of the view down the river. In this direction, about a mile upstream, is a famous fourteenth - century hermitage, a dwelling of several chambers and a chapel, hewn out of solid rock. In the other direction the view from the castle and the green space below it is down the returning loop of the river to Amble, the sea, and the white lighthouse of Coquet Island.

Whalton (23). A good village of many large houses and brown stone cottages facing on to fine trees and greens. At the east end is the Manor House which was made into such, in

1908, by Sir Edwin Lutyens converting four village houses into one Lutyenesque building. The good church is mainly thirteenth century; and the rectory incorporates part of a peel-tower.

They burn the Bale here at pub-closing time on July 4th. There are mounds of two earthworks along the Morpeth road, by Camp Hill Farm, one called Dead Men's Graves.

West Woodburn (12). A plain long steeply falling-and-rising village on the present line of Dere Street, of no special character but useful to travellers as probably the only place offering food and accommodation on the long stretch this way from Corbridge by Carter Bar to Jedburgh (though Otterburn is only five miles off). The church of 1906, by Hicks and Charlewood, is a nice building with a pretty octagonal bell-turret. The old Dere Street crossed the Rede a little to the west; and there in the fields is the mound and some of the wall of the Roman fort of Risingham (Habitancum).

Two miles up the road northwards, a field or two back on the right-hand side, are the small grey church of *Corsenside* and its rectory, standing oddly and touchingly alone among rolling hills. The church is basically Norman, but was largely rebuilt in 1810, with domestic-looking windows. The rectory, now a farmhouse, has the date 1680 above its door.

Whitfield (17). Scattered farmsteads and cottages among trees, part on the banks of the West Allen, part on its tributary the East Allen, in perhaps the most beautiful locality in all Northumberland: embowered in splendid trees and parkland. There are two churches—one, the "old" church, St John, Georgian with Victorian alterations, tucked away off the main road: the other, wholly Victorian (1860) with a spire and some surprisingly pleasant glass. The Hall is of 1750–60, with a storey added in 1856. To the north-east (1½ miles) is Cupola Bridge (but no cupola visible) where the two Allens meet under cliffs, and the road hairpins up Grindstone Elbow from the top of which the tower of Staward Peel can be seen among the replanted trees of the river ravine.

Morwick water tower, near WARKWORTH

TYNEMOUTH Castle and Priory

Whitley Bay (24). Beside the seaside. On the sea-front, miles-long promenades, boarding houses, sands, lawns, rock gardens and fun fairs. Masses of streets behind, stretching back to include Monkseaton. A lot of Newcastle business people live here: and it is popular with Scots on holiday. The lighthouse on St Mary's Island (an island only at high tide) makes an eye-catching feature on the north.

WHALTON

Whittingham (8). A well-situated and pleasant village not far from the edge of the Cheviots, backed by bumpy little hills, and divided by the tree-bordered infant Aln into two parallel parts, one with a green and fine trees, the other without. The largely late-Saxon church was badly hacked about in restorations beginning with one in 1840 when the upper part of the Saxon tower was blown up to make bigger and better Gothic, and

Norman piers were knocked down and replaced by imitation late thirteenth-century work. But it still has a lot of character and is a well-cared-for church. Whittingham Tower, a fifteenth-century peel was restored and converted into almshouses for old ladies in 1845. There is a well-known fair here in August.

Callaly Castle (1½ miles south) is a fine large interesting house of various periods harmoniously

Callaly Castle, near WHITTINGHAM

blended. Beginning as a medieval tower, extended (probably by Trollope) in 1676, again in 1707, 1727, 1750, 1835 and 1890, it manages splendidly to retain one character, essentially classical. There are the scanty remains of two earlier castles near by.

Eslington Hall (2 miles west) is a large stone mansion of about 1720 in grounds with fine trees.

At Thrunton Farm (1 mile southeast) Bronze Age relics were found in 1847.

Whittonstall (25). A hamlet on high ground near the Durham boundary, with a church of 1830 by Jonathan Marshall.

Widdrington (25). The old village of Widdrington has disappeared, as has the later mining one: and nothing remains either of the castle (pulled down about 1775) associated with the family of which one famous member is immortalized in the lines

of the ballad of Chevy Chase:

For Wetharryngton my harte was
                                            wo,
That ever he slayne shulde be;
For when both his leggis were
                            hewyne in to
Ywt he knyled and fought on hys
                                            kne.

But the fine little church remains, partly late-Norman, partly fourteenth century, standing in a walled churchyard in a walled field.

Woodhorn (21). A mining village near the sea with a good church standing in an overgrown and over-treed churchyard. The church, though it was restored in 1842, has Norman, thirteenth- and fourteenth-century work: also a very good thirteenth-century effigy of a lady, and a nice relief of 1807 and others of 1828 and 1830.

Wooler (5). A mostly nineteenth-century hillside market and holiday town without much character but

well situated under Cheviot for seeing that country. The church has an eighteenth-century interior (1765) and a Victorian exterior (mostly 1873). The Roman Catholic church is of *c.* 1850. There is the mound of a Norman motte-and-bailey, and on it some rubble remains of an early sixteenth-century tower. Although the town is not much in itself, it looks well, stepping up on its hill, when seen from outside.

On Coldmartin Hill to the east are a little lough, a ruined peel and a tower. To the south-west an old earthwork known as The Kettles. To the north, about the hamlet of Humbleton, other earthworks; and the Battle Stone commemorating the great battle of Humbleton or Homildon Hill fought between English and Scots in 1402.

Beyond that, at *Akeld*, are the ruins of a fifteenth-century bastel-

Callaly Castle

Shipbuilding at WALLSEND

house, the massive ramparts of a promontory fort on Harehope Hill, of another at Gleadsclough and the remains of no less than nine hill forts, eleven high-ground forts, five valley forts, and numerous hut circles round about.

Wooperton (8). A hamlet under Hedgehope and Cheviot. In the fields

to the south was fought the battle of Hedgeley Moor, between the Yorkist and Lancastrian armies, in 1464. In a little walled enclosure beside the main road there is the tall shaft of a now headless cross marking the place where the Percy leader of the Lancastrians was killed.

Wylam (23). A substantial village on

the north bank of the Tyne. Its principal fame is as the birthplace of George Stephenson, the great railway engineer, in 1781. The cottage where he was born is the property of the National Trust. The church is of 1886; the Hall, incorporating medieval work, is mainly of *c.* 1880; and there is a good house (Close House) of 1779.

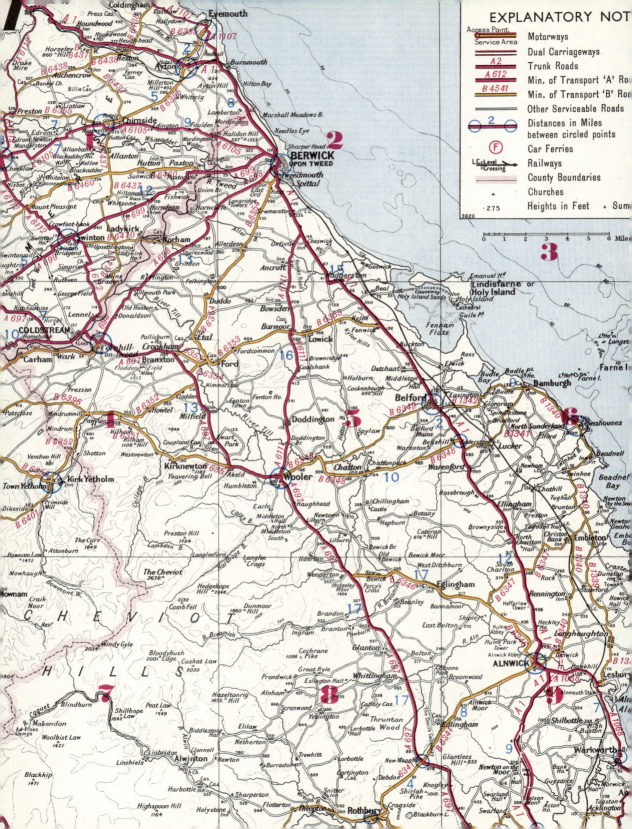

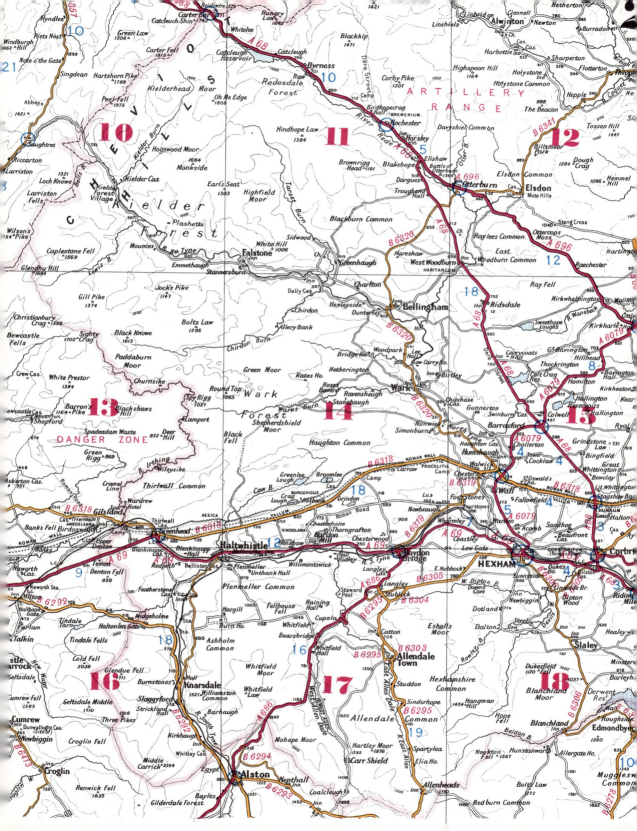

INDEX

ROTHBURY